If I Can You Can

Law of Attraction and Synchronicity in action

Matt Parsons

Copyright © 2022 Matthew Parsons

All rights reserved.

ISBN: 9798843765835

DEDICATION

This book is dedicated to my family.

CONTENTS

Introduction	Who am I and what makes this book different?	1
Chapter 1	Setting the scene – Finding my perfect job	6
Chapter 2	Finding love	21
Chapter 3	Life is a game	41
Chapter 4	Time is just an illusion	46
Chapter 5	Tune into the right frequency	53
Chapter 6	The music dream	62
Chapter 7	Open the doors	68
Chapter 8	More doors of synchronicity – Accept and adapt	76
Chapter 9	Understanding emotions	85
Chapter 10	Self-motivation	91
Chapter 11	Do you trust your parking sensors?	99
Chapter 12	You are a very rich young man	104
Chapter 13	Following creativity	110
Chapter 14	Use of language	114
Chapter 15	Dr Joe Vitale – Inspired action	120
Chapter 16	Living out my childhood dream	130
Chapter 17	Toxicity	137
Chapter 18	Forgiveness	147

Chapter 19	Self-love	153
Chapter 20	Notice the signs	160
Chapter 21	The day my life changed	165
Chapter 22	A shattered dream	178
Chapter 23	Luck or chance?	190
Chapter 24	Staying true to yourself?	194
Chapter 25	If I can, you can	201
Chapter 26	Exercises to try	210
	Bibliography	219
	About the Author	220

ACKNOWLEDGMENTS

Thank you to my family for your endless love and support, especially my beautiful wife Kate. Thank you to Gill Press, Kevin Ward, Louise Pigott for your kind generosity. Finally, thank you to Dr Joe Vitale for your teachings and inspiration. Without your words of wisdom, this book would never have been written.

INTRODUCTION
WHO AM I AND WHAT MAKES THIS BOOK DIFFERENT?

Thank you for picking up this book. My name is Matt Parsons. I'm an ordinary guy who, like everyone, has been through some good times and some bad times. But along the way I've noticed how the Law of Attraction and Synchronicity can work together when manifesting anything in your life. I'm writing this book because over the years I have developed tips and techniques to happiness. I want you to be happy. I want everyone to be happy. Every single person on this planet deserves happiness. We were born to love and to experience this wonderful planet. We were not born to suffer. That being said, I was born with a disability called Erb's Palsy / Brachial Plexus Injury in my left arm. Erb's Palsy, is a condition which mainly due to birth trauma can affect one or all of the five primary nerves that supply the movement and feeling to an arm. Each baby's injury is individual. The paralysis can be partial or complete; the damage to each nerve can range from bruising to tearing. Some babies recover on their own; however, some may require specialist intervention. For many people this is a life-long disability which can affect the mobility and function of their arm, and impact upon their daily life.

Living with this injury has opened many doors for me and I have met some wonderful people along the way. I am totally grateful to have been born with it. It wasn't easy getting to the point of complete acceptance, but when I worked out how synchronistic events unfolded throughout my life, to get me where I am now, I can't help but be happy and grateful.

I decided to write this book to document my journey, with the hope that it inspires you and helps you reflect on your own life experiences. I believe it's important to look back at what we've done, make peace with it, learn from it and move forward positively, with the aim to be the best version of ourselves that we can be. I didn't write this book to show off in any way. I'm not gloating about my life, so please don't think that. Through my own self-discovery I have learned a lot about how the Universe can help you achieve your hopes and dreams. If you read on, I will show you ways that you can bring joy, love and happiness into your life. At the end of the day, that is all we want.

What is the Law of Attraction? Simply put, the Law of Attraction means whatever you think about, you bring about. Whatever you give your energy to, you will attract. It sounds pretty simple, but there is much more to it than that. It's not as straightforward as writing down what you want, then sitting down and waiting for it to fall into your lap. The Law of Attraction is a real thing. I'm writing this book to give you real life examples of how I have used it in my life, both willingly and unwillingly. If you've not heard about the Law of Attraction, I suggest reading The Secret by Rhonda Byrne, The Attractor Factor by Dr Joe Vitale, and Ask and It Is Given by Esther and Jerry Hicks. There are many more books and courses out there, but these would certainly be a good starting point.

What is Synchronicity? Synchronicities are those chance meetings. The coincidences that appear in our life that lead us somewhere magical. The more we see them and acknowledge them, the more they happen to us. I learned about Synchronicity through reading The Celestine Prophecy by James Redfield and The 7 Secrets of Synchronicity by Trish Macgregor and Rob Macgregor. I subsequently read many books to help me understand how it worked.

Although I'm a normal guy, living a normal life, I have attracted some pretty extraordinary things, which I'm excited to share with you. I have come to notice how Synchronicity is always working and the more we notice these coincidences, the more they happen. Life is an incredible journey and I feel very lucky to be here writing this book. Through sharing my stories, I will show you real life examples of inspired action and how it can open many doors for you. I also hope to open your eyes and show you that the power of the Universe is a real thing and that you are the biggest player in this amazing game of life.

Many of us have been in a situation where we know we need to make a change in our life. We head to our local bookshop to find a book that can help us. We may put an audiobook on, so that we can absorb positive messages when we are on the way to work. We try to monitor our thoughts and visualise, yet we are still stuck in a rut. I've been there. I know exactly how it feels. Am I sitting here writing this claiming that my life is perfect? Not at all, but it's damn close. I believe that I am successful. We all have different ideas of success. Many of the self-help books we buy give us the idea that we need to be a millionaire, or a celebrity to be successful. I'm sure for many people this is still their idea of success, but I've come to learn than success is what WE define it to be. The official definition of success is "The accomplishment of an aim or purpose." Unfortunately, we compare our success to that of others. We can lose sight of WHY we are setting the goal in the first place. Looking deeper, it's important to understand that the Universe is working with you. Sometimes the Universe delivers to you in the most unpredictable of ways. When we get our ego out of the way, release the need to control and actually allow the Universe to help us, then wonderful things can happen.

This book is full of my personal experiences with the Law of Attraction and Synchronicity. If you are familiar with both of these things, then hopefully this book will solidify your faith. For those of you who are new to the ideas, I hope that they inspire you in some way and help you realise your own potential. I also hope that by reading this book you will remain open minded and know that these are just my experiences. Many people across the world have manifested incredible things in their life. Am I any different? Not especially. We are all connected, and we are all able to manifest our dreams. I guess one thing that is a little more unique is my Erb's Palsy. During this book I explain the Synchronicity behind this "disability" and tell you how I overcame the odds. I talk about how I have attracted my perfect job, relationship and dream car. I have also manifested things that I didn't want! It's important to explore why this has happened so that I don't make the same mistakes again. As mentioned previously, in no way do I wish to brag about my life. I took inspired action, with an aim to bring some good into my life. The Law of Attraction isn't just about attracting materialistic possessions. It's about being happy, being clear and connecting with the divine.

CHAPTER ONE
SETTING THE SCENE – FINDING THE PERFECT JOB

I'm a secondary school teacher. I teach 11–18-year-olds and I specialise in Design Technology. I LOVE creativity and I love seeing my pupils excel in my subject. It's an interesting coincidence how all this came to be. I don't have a degree in Design Technology. My degree is actually in Fine Art. Some people think it's strange that I teach Design Technology, specialising in woods, metals, plastics, CAD / CAM (Computer Aided Design / Computer Aided Manufacture) and graphics, when I studied painting, drawing, photography and a little bit of film during my university life. My mother always said that I'd make a great teacher, but like most teenagers, I didn't listen to my parents. I wanted to explore things a little more. I've always had an entrepreneurial mindset and I love trying new things. I have so many hobbies and interests that it can be tricky to juggle them at times, but I do what I'm guided to do. I listen to my inner voice and act on the nudges that I get. Doing this led me to a pretty wonderful place.

When I pictured my life and the job I wanted to do, I initially saw myself as a property developer. I purchased a house with a 5% deposit after graduating from university in 2006. The deposit was only £3750. I renovated it and made a little bit of profit. I thought that this would be a good way to get rich young and live out my wildest dreams. Teaching was certainly not on the agenda. In fact, it couldn't have been further away from my dream job. I have a passion for music, so I recorded an album and decided I wanted to be a musician in the hopes that I could tour the world and become rich and famous. I then wanted to be an author, so I wrote a short book. I decided I wanted to buy property overseas, so bought an apartment on a golf course on a new and exciting development. I then thought it would be a good idea to go into business with my dad, selling sporting equipment online. Looking back at all of these ventures, I now realise that I was chasing money. I wanted to be rich, admired and feel powerful. I wanted to be able to buy what I wanted and do what I wanted, whenever I wanted. It turns out that I didn't become a property developer. I didn't become a famous musician or author (yet). I lost a lot of money overseas and sadly the business I started with my dad wasn't very profitable and we lost money and ended up owing a lot too.

At this point you may wonder why I'm writing a book about my experiences with the Law of Attraction and Synchronicity! It sure doesn't sound like I'm doing very well at manifesting my desires. All those things happened for a reason. Those experiences got me to where I am today. I am so happy. I'm not a millionaire, I'm no longer chasing money, yet I have everything I need. You may ask WHY I am not a millionaire, well I'll get to that later. What I didn't realise at the time was that the Universe was speaking to me, but I was ignoring it. The Universe was constantly giving me signs and nudges, but I was so fixed on what I wanted to do, I missed all of the other opportunities. It took me a long time to work this out and when I did, it changed every aspect of my life.

I was walking down the stairs the other day and the stair gate on the bottom step was open. We keep it closed for our son and for our dog Juno. We don't allow Juno upstairs. However, when she does see the gate open, she runs up as fast as she can, jumps on the bed and refuses to get down. Juno is a Beagle and she is driven by food. My wife Kate was feeding her. Juno was so fixed on the food that she missed a golden opportunity to go upstairs. I was like Juno with my goals! I was so fixed on the goal that I wasn't seeing the other opportunities. I wasn't allowing myself to see them. I was acting from ego and a desire to be rich. In my head, this way was the only way. I wasn't really listening to the inner nudge. Something I have now learnt to listen to and act upon all the time.

So how did I end up as a teacher I hear you ask? I also hear you ask; How come you had all of these ideas and you ended up in the classroom? Well, it's an interesting story which is full of experiences and tales of the Law of Attraction and Synchronicity. To tell it I need to take you back twelve years. I mentioned earlier that I ran a business with my father selling sporting goods. My father would go out on the road to get sales with trade customers, and I developed the online side of the business. I ran the eBay and Amazon shop and developed the website. Growing up I often heard my parents arguing about money. When I was a young boy, I remember hiding behind the sofa so that the bailiffs didn't see us and take our possessions away when my dad's first business went bankrupt. I remember one Christmas Eve when I was in bed, my mum came into my room and said, "we can't really afford to get you much this year." I really didn't care. I'm not one for wanting huge presents, but for some reason it made me feel bad. Times were tough. My dad would get up early and go out to work, come home and go out taxi driving until the early hours. My mum would sell her artwork too. We got by and eventually things got better. Unfortunately, the business I started with my dad didn't do as we expected. This sparked up the old fears of money and somehow, we were really struggling again. We owed a lot of money. I needed a job and I needed one quickly. My brother-in-law is a builder and I asked him if he knew of any labouring jobs. He didn't know of any, but he did say that there was a job coming up at the local Howdens branch as a counter boy (Howdens sells kitchens, doors and skirting boards and have many branches across the UK).

I went to visit the local branch and by pure "luck", the manager and one of the kitchen designers both went to my old school. The kitchen designer also played cricket with me for the local village club. I had no idea he worked there. I put a CV together, had an interview the next day and got the job there and then. That was the first Synchronicity that I experienced, but at the time I had no idea what a Synchronicity was. I worked on the counter every day selling door hinges, skirting boards, doors and trying to get leads for the kitchen designers. To be honest I had no idea what I was talking about, and this really frustrated a lot of the builders who came in. I tried my best and I was grateful to have a payslip coming in every month. It was by no means a huge amount of money, but it was just about paying my bills. After a while my manager decided to promote me to a kitchen designer. This was an amazing opportunity for me. Within six months working there, I had been promoted. I was learning new skills and I had a slight pay increase. I really enjoyed the design aspect to the job. I loved meeting new people, going out to different houses, measuring the rooms, and then going back to the office to make a CAD render of the new design. This was a cool job. After a while though, I discovered the pressure of being in sales. It wasn't about the designing. It was about hitting targets. The financial weight of the branch was on the shoulders of the two kitchen designers, as we brought in the most money each month. It became a tough job and my relationship with the manager changed.

I mentioned earlier that I always come up with ideas. At that point I was still gigging a little and I thought that I could break away from the pressure of sales by working as a full-time musician. If I could get paid £200 per night to do a gig, I would only need to do two gigs per week to make the same amount of money as I would as a kitchen designer. A friend at the time was also breaking free from the 9-5 life. He became a blogger and was earning good money. He gave me some tips and I set up my own blog documenting my plan about breaking free and becoming an independent musician. One day I wrote a post about my intentions to leave my full-time job in twelve months and do the thing that I loved the most. I also mentioned how I was frustrated at work and the best way to get me motivated isn't to make me feel like shit. I tweeted my blog and ten minutes later my boss 'liked' it. My heart sank. I realised that he read that I was planning to leave my job and that he makes me feel like shit. I deleted the post instantly and went into work with the aim to ignore it. An hour into work, he called me into his office. Looking back now I know he was trying to make me sweat, but at the time I was panicking and I broke down in tears. I NEEDED a job. I NEEDED money and he knew this too. He said that I had broken some part of my contract and that he'd spoken to the area manager, and he would make the decision by the end of the day if I'd keep my job or not. I felt awful. He called me into his office an hour before we closed for the day and said that the area manager told him that I could keep my job. I know now that he was playing a game. He wanted to punish me and show me who was boss. I went home and deleted my blog and never wrote another article. He had proven his point. He had won.

Several months later, I was playing a gig in my hometown, and I bumped into an old school friend called Nick. It was a huge coincidence as he was actually living in Hong Kong and was only back in the UK for a short while. We had a drink together and I was telling him about gigs that I'd done for charity and the album I'd put together. I didn't really think anything of it as it was general chit chat. We finished our drinks and said farewell. Around two months later I was in the same pub and Nick walked in again. I couldn't believe it. Once again we chatted, and he told me that he was on the committee for old pupils at the school we both went to. He went on to say that there was a big event coming up and the Headmaster was looking for a guest speaker. He asked me if I wanted to do it. I don't even remember thinking about it. I just said yes there and then. I wrote a speech and delivered it a few months later. It was great to be back in my old school. I had some very fond memories of my time there, and I had developed some lifelong friends. After the speech the Headmaster came over, praised me and thanked me for taking time out of my day to come into the school. We had lunch together and got on really well. At the time I was looking at doing a teacher training course. I knew I didn't want to stay as a kitchen designer, so I was thinking about other job options. During a conversation with him, I happened to say that I was looking at teacher training courses, but I didn't think anything of it. I went back to work, kept my head down and tried to reach all of my monthly targets. One week later, I received a voicemail from the Headmaster. It said, "Hi Matt, please could you give me a call. There's a job opportunity at school which I think you might be interested in." I phoned him back straight away. The job was a one-year post as a teaching assistant. He explained that if I took the job, they would look at training me up to be a teacher if I proved that I was good enough. I knew in my heart that this was meant to be. There was zero doubt. I had an interview one week later and I got the job. I took great pleasure handing my notice in to my manager. I left two weeks later and never looked back. The environment became very difficult to be in and after the way I was treated by my manager, I knew I deserved better.

All of this was Synchronicity in action. What were the chances of me getting the job at Howdens in the first place? Especially with the first phone call applying for jobs. I also knew two people who worked there. When I wanted to change jobs, I started looking at teacher training courses. I randomly bumped into an old school friend who gave me the opportunity to deliver a speech. He didn't know I was thinking of becoming a teacher. All of this is a combination of the Law of Attraction and Synchronicity. I set an intention and I was taking the opportunities when they were presented to me. I was also making opportunities, by setting the intentions in the first place. But the story doesn't end there...

During this time, I was engaged to a woman who will remain nameless. We owned a house together, but things weren't going well. The financial situation of the business was taking its toll and the stresses of our individual jobs didn't help either. We were arguing a lot and we ended up calling the wedding off and several complicated months later we broke up. There's a lot more to the story of this relationship, but I won't go into that right now. Looking back, she was the person who introduced me to Synchronicity. She gave me a book called 'The Celestine Prophecy' by James Redfield. It totally changed my life. She also introduced me to 'Fabric of the Cosmos' by Brian Greene. If nothing else, this was a reason that we got together. Both of these books have had a profound effect on me and changed the way that I view the world. So, for that I am forever grateful.

I accepted the job as a teaching assistant. I was inspired and excited to be given this opportunity and I couldn't wait to start. The job didn't pay much at all, but they offered me free accommodation and food. I had just broken up with my fiancé, so I needed somewhere to live (another Synchronicity). We had a pretty big argument about it, because I took the job without talking to her about it. We still had a mortgage, but we had a house mate who would make up the financial difference. Thinking about it now, I definitely should have spoken to her about it, but I knew in my heart that I had to take this job. What if she said I couldn't take it? Besides, we weren't together anymore, and we were going to sell the house.

As I left, I got into my car and drove into my new life. It was one of the most surreal things I've experienced. I remember not looking back and I could sense a golden rainbow over me as I drove through it. I felt that I was leaving negativity behind and driving into a new life that was destined for me. It sounds crazy I know, but it was a very real experience. I still owed money on my credit cards, and I wanted to pay this off as soon as I could. I didn't know how I would do this, but I started putting a plan into place. We put the house on the market, and it sold within a week. We only owned the house for 18 months, but we made almost £20000. We split it 50/50 and it paid off my personal credit cards.

I really enjoyed my first year as a teaching assistant. I was given the opportunity to lead some lessons and I gained more responsibility as the year progressed. I managed to secure a contract for another year, but I had pretty much a full teaching timetable, even though I was unqualified. The year after that the school paid £6000 for my teaching qualification. I could learn and qualify while on the job and I didn't need to pay a penny back. I knew deep down that this was the right job for me. In the past, I always felt that I was struggling and that there was something more for me to do. I felt like I had a purpose and I found it when I took this job. A series of Synchronicities led me there. I acted on my instincts and through my actions, I noticed more coincidences, which subsequently opened the doors to where I belong.

As the years passed my feelings towards the school changed. My relationships were also changing with my colleagues, and it didn't have the same positivity that it did at the beginning. I've learned that I must act when I get these feelings. I went for a promotion to see if that would change things. My "dream job role" presented itself and I thought I was destined to have it. I should have learned that deep down it wasn't right. The job was for a pastoral middle leader role. I read every policy and prepared answers to hundreds of questions. When I had the interview, it felt awkward and for some reason I felt that I had no chance of getting it and that they had already made their minds up of who they wanted. I KNEW I could do this job though. I didn't get the job and I was devastated. I was also deeply hurt by the way I was treated after it. I won't go into details, but I instantly looked at jobs at other schools. Maybe I was still holding on to the feelings of how my manager treated me when I was a kitchen designer. I knew I deserved more.

One day there was a Design Technology job advertised at the school that my father went to as a boy in the 1960's. I applied for the job, but I also knew that there was an opportunity coming up at the school my next-door neighbour works at. I went to the interview not thinking too much about it and I thought, "even if I don't get it, it's still good practice." It turned out I was the only candidate being interviewed. I fell in love with the place instantly. The ethos was brilliant, and it didn't need to show off in any way. It just sold itself. I was offered the job and I accepted it without question. It came at the perfect time. It also turned out that the job I thought was coming up at the other school didn't materialise in the end, so it worked out perfectly.

I started the job in May 2020 at a difficult time. Schools across the country were being closed and pupils were learning at home online, due to Covid-19. Despite this, I felt a part of the team right away and I loved my new department. Less than a year into my new role, a pastoral middle leader position came up, so I applied. I prepared myself as much as I could, and I was offered the job. It was advertised as an "acting Head of Year" due to school restructures, but I was over the moon to be given the opportunity. A few months later, my Head of Department announced that he was retiring at the end of the academic year. An advert for the job came out and I had the feeling in my heart (similar to the one I had when the teaching assistant job came up) that I had to apply for it. It was strange, because I had just been given a position as a Head of Year and then this turned up. I applied for the position, and I was successful.

It goes to show that change is so important. We are terrified of change, and we worry that we may make the wrong decision. Subconscious limiting beliefs and doubts can control us and make us say things like "the grass isn't always greener on the other side." In fact, when I was applying for the job at the new school, some of my old colleagues actually said that to me! They were trying to hold me back. They were pointing out all of the negatives to me, rather than being happy that this could be a really good change for me. It turned out that this was an incredible change and I'm so happy in my job right now.

So why am I not a millionaire? I can attract jobs. Why am I not telling you about how I attracted lots and lots of money? Well, I love my job. I love teaching and I love having a positive impact on my pupils' lives. Yes, I've had dreams of being a millionaire. I've tried to attract winning the lottery, but every time I do that, I believe in my heart that I'm exactly where I'm meant to be. I went through a stage of winning small amounts regularly, but it took a lot of effort for not a lot of money. I would also rather be a self-made millionaire rather than winning millions overnight. There is more of a sense of purpose and appreciation for the money. I've listened and acted on the nudges from the Universe, and it has led me to this exact moment. I've noticed the synchronicities and they have led me to some wonderful situations. I am truly happy. I earn a decent wage; I have a lovely four bed detached house. I have a beautiful wife and family. I have a car and I am truly blessed. I can afford to buy what I need, and we go on nice holidays.

Could I have more? I could have more money, I guess. But I have decided NOT to chase money. Money will come to me. I have so much love in my life. I feel it at home, and I feel it at work. Right now, this is where I'm meant to be. As I'm writing this, I have no idea where the future will take me. I had no idea that when I decided I wanted to be a property developer, I would then want to be a musician. This led me to starting a business, to being a kitchen designer and then to being a teacher. I follow my instincts, which is something we have forgotten how to do and something many of us don't trust. We like to feel in control. We like to know HOW and WHY, but we don't need to know those details. The Universe is giving us everything and the signs are there, we just need to let them in, notice them, trust and act.

Before I end this chapter, I want to tell you one more story about my job. I practice mindfulness as much as I can, and I know the benefits of making it a part of your life. When I was on my teacher training course, I listened to a talk from a lady who spoke about the amazing Mindfulness in Schools Project. She delivered an 8-week course to her pupils called "dot-be". I was really interested in this, so I spoke to her after the event. She gave me all of the information, plus a copy of a mindfulness journal that she put together for the pupils. As soon as I got home, I started to do some research.

I sent an email right away to a member of leadership and explained that I had found a way to help reduce our pupils anxiety, stress, anger, help their concentration and learn to love and accept themselves. We booked in a meeting, and I told him all about it. He asked me to put a 5-year development plan together and then deliver it to all members of senior leadership. This was very intimidating, but I did it. I spent weeks putting this proposal together, but sadly they did not buy into it. Mindfulness was too close to prayer and working in a Catholic school it didn't fit with their beliefs. They also said that they didn't have time to fit it into the school structure, even though I planned everything out. They asked me to trial a co-curricular club, but said that it had been done before and not many people went. Talk about crushing a dream. Regardless, I started the club, and I had a few regular pupils who certainly benefited from it.

Six months after I started the job at my new school I was asked to go on the Mindfulness in Schools "dot-be" training course. I couldn't believe it. I was working so hard to try to introduce this to my last school and within six months of my new job I was asked to go on it. Another strange Synchronicity happened here too. When I originally pitched the idea to the school, a member of leadership gave me a name of a person who works at my current school. I had no idea that I would ever end up working there. He told me that he runs the mindfulness course and they have managed to build it into the curriculum. I emailed him straight away and organised a phone call. He was a lovely man, and we had an in-depth conversation, and I based my 5-year plan on what he had said. If it worked in his school, it could work in mine. A few years later, I am now friends with that man and although we teach different subjects, we play golf, co-teach the "Extended Project Qualification" and run a hockey team together. We even play cricket and play guitar and sing. To think that I would work at the same school and then have all the same interests as him, would never have crossed my mind. This is definitely another example of one of the many "coincidences" that have happened in my life.

For some, this may be seen as luck. Some may even read this and think that it's not a big deal. What I hope you understand from these stories is that I was setting intentions, following my intuition, and using inspired action. As I did this, the Law of Attraction was working and more synchronicities occurred. We don't need to be mega rich to be successful. Of course, having an abundance of money is a form of success, but it's not everything. I live a happy and fulfilling life and I have a job that feels right. We all have our "thing" and my thing, for now is teaching. In the time that I've been a teacher I've met my wife, been trained for free, learned how to ski, learned a huge range of new skills, been on trips to France, Spain, Ecuador, Italy, Galapagos, Austria and more. I would never have had any of that if I didn't act on my intuition.

ACTION POINTS

- Trust your instincts
- Use inspired action
- Notice "coincidences" and act on them

CHAPTER TWO
FINDING LOVE

During the first couple of years working in my new profession I dated a fair amount. I let my hair down, but I was confused and emotionally drained. I had just called off a wedding, split up with my fiancé and sold our house. I wasn't really in the best place to date, but I wanted to be with someone. I wanted some company to fill the empty space. I would either really like someone, but they didn't like me, or the other way around. I dated some really lovely people, but at the time I felt broken. Because of the way things ended with my ex-fiancé, my insecurities were running wild. In my head I couldn't commit, and I always felt bad for how things ended. It didn't feel right to start a relationship when I was feeling this way. I also got a little bit tired of looking for love. I wanted to feel happy by myself. I didn't want someone else to make me happy. I think it's hugely important to have your own energy and not drain your partners and have an expectation that they to give it to you. It's your responsibility to fix any issues within yourself. That is your job and your job alone. It was New Year's

Eve 2014 and I decided that this was going to be my last wild night out. It was also my last night of eating meat. Something inside me was telling me to become a vegetarian. I don't know why, but it did. I listened to the voice, and I've not eaten meat since. I decided that from January 1st 2015, I would focus on myself and not to go looking for love. I had always wanted to find my soul mate. I thought that I had an image of what that would look like, but often with these things, they don't pan out how you expect them to.

I remember clearly during my first year working as a teaching assistant, I took myself off for an evening walk in the beautiful grounds of the school. I sat in the middle of one of the cricket pitches, which was on top of a hill, looking down into the beautiful countryside. I sat there listening to a stunning album by an artist called Dan Arborise. As I sat there, enchanted by this music I started to FEEL love. I felt love in every part of my body. I felt what it actually feels like to be deeply in love with someone. I started to cry. I had found my soulmate. I was so happy, but at that moment I was all alone in a field and couldn't have been further away from it. What I'd unconsciously done was send out a clear feeling to the Universe of what I wanted. The Universe doesn't really understand language like we do. That's why prayer is so powerful, because when we pray, we FEEL what we are saying, and we are sending that feeling out to the those around us and beyond. It's the same when we visualise or repeat affirmations. Feeling something with all of your might is very powerful and it's something that is wonderful about being human. The ability to emotionally feel is incredibly important for both manifesting and understanding who you are.

You can tell this when someone delivers a speech or sings a song. There's a difference between someone just saying or singing the words and saying them or singing them with feeling! When you believe the words that you are saying, it supports the feelings you have, and the Universe therefore understands what you want and starts working at bringing your desires to you. I had no idea what was working behind the scenes for me.

Many of us wonder if we will ever find "The One." Some people don't believe that "The One" exists and that we shouldn't be tied to just one person for the rest of our lives. To start with, the idea of being "tied to someone" is hugely negative and if you think like that, then your relationship certainly won't be free or healthy. Some people simply don't care about finding the one. Some people have been searching for them for so long, it becomes more of a burden than exciting for them.

Let's look at the facts. There are approximately 8 billion people in the world. The chances of finding someone you love is huge. It's a big world out there. Often, we end up staying in our small circle of friends. We go to work and then come home. Sometimes we may join an evening class or go to the gym, often in hopes that we bump into someone and instantly fall in love with them, just like we see in the movies. The truth is, from my experience, it doesn't always happen like that. Personally, I found that meeting people in a bar or online didn't really work for me. I know there are millions of people out there that it has worked for and that is so wonderful. But for me it was very different.

I loved the idea of "The One" ever since I was a teenager. In fact, when I was 17, I went out with a girl for almost three years, and we were convinced that we were going to get married. We didn't get married, and as sweet as she was, I'm really glad that we broke up. I've had quite a number of relationships over the years. Some have been very intense, and some have been pretty relaxed. Some have been long, and some have been short. There were times that I was trying to convince myself that the person I was with was the one. I knew deep down that this wasn't the case, but I still tried to make it work. This then caused a lot of pressures on the relationship because I was trying to make it something it wasn't.

During the times that I was single I would be constantly looking at people to see if I get that magical moment when you instantly know you are meant to be together. The more I looked, the harder it became. I have dated some lovely people and I have certainly fallen in love with some of them. But I knew deep down that it wasn't right. I had a feeling in my stomach that told me I needed to leave. I often ignored it and tried to make it work anyway, but this only led to more heartache for both people.

I decided to completely give up. I managed to get to a place where I was totally happy with being on my own. I decided that I wasn't going to date anybody, and I didn't even want anything casual. It all became about me and my life. I took myself on trips abroad and weekend trips in my campervan and I didn't look at anyone in a lustful way. If there were any signs of flirtation, I would play along, but not talk myself into the fact that I had to fall in love with this person. It was actually a really nice place to be. There was a weight that lifted and the clouds that hung over had cleared.

Why did I want to find "The One"? I wanted to be loved. I wanted someone to adore me, and I wanted to adore them. Deep down I wanted that because I didn't accept myself for who I was. If someone else loved me, I wouldn't have to love myself. This is completely the wrong way of looking at love. Loving yourself first is the key. It allows you to come into a relationship with fewer insecurities and a place of complete love and acceptance. It also helps manifest relationships because if you are around someone who is comfortable with who they are, it is so much more relaxing and enjoyable.

While all of this was going on I was building a really strong friendship with a woman from work. I had not looked at her in a romantic way before. We just enjoyed each other's company and had a laugh together. As the months passed, we were spending most weekends together and even staying over each other's houses, just watching movies, drinking wine, and eating popcorn. She had been giving me advice about my dating life and I was doing the same for her. One night we were watching a movie in her bedroom, and we cuddled up. The movie finished and we just stayed there for hours. I felt so completely at peace and after a long battle in my head as to whether I should kiss her or not, I decided to go for it. This was a bold move considering we were close friends, we worked together and that I had given up on dating.

Was it a really passionate, love at first kiss, like you see in movies moment? No. To be honest it was a little awkward. Nevertheless, we kept hanging out and we were completely open and honest about how we felt about the situation. We both loved each other's company and if we both decided to go for it, then that would be it. No messing around. In retrospect, what happened is that we realised we actually loved each other, but as we were both not looking for love and we were not interested in sex at the time, we just fell in love based on our personalities and an incredible friendship. We got married 18 months later and now we have two wonderful children.

The strange thing was that on paper, we aren't necessarily the perfect match. When I was online dating, I would scroll through the photos and dismiss people who were probably wonderful. We put so much emphasis on the 'love at first sight' experience, that we are led to believe will happen. The wonderful thing about our relationship is that we are fundamentally friends, who make each other laugh and want to be with all of the time. However, I understand that this may not suit everyone, and I completely understand why. We both have our own individual hobbies, which is so important as we need to keep our own identities.

I attracted my wife. Not in a physical, lustful way though. I knew what I wanted out of a relationship, and I put it out there to the Universe. When I sat on the top of the hill and cried tears of joy for FEELING love and finding my soul mate, I triggered something. The Universe knew exactly what I wanted and started to work for me. Coincidences started to occur to line us up. We started going to some of the same parties and work events. My wife teaches Spanish and a little French. I was asked to go on a school trip to France as they needed another male member of staff. This was when we started to become friends. At this point we had no idea we would end up married. We didn't look at each other that way. One of the guys I was sharing a house with at the time was dating her and the thought never crossed my mind. All these events were not coincidence. They happened to make sure that it lined up for us. After all the searching for love and my soul mate, she was hidden right in front of me. I was looking everywhere, except right in front of my eyes. To allow the Universe to deliver, you need to let go and trust that it will deliver. And believe me, it delivered. It wasn't until one day that I actually listened and followed my inner nudge that we opened the doors into a beautiful new relationship, and we realised that we had found one another.

Finding the one will be different for everyone, but I do believe that they exist. You could argue that not everyone is destined to find somebody. Some people don't even want a relationship and that is fine. I know that what I have with my wife is incredible and I couldn't imagine a relationship with someone else being any better.

The key is to listen to what your instinct is telling you. If your gut or intuition is saying something isn't right, then you must listen and act on that. There's no point in wasting time, energy and emotion on something that isn't going to work. Yes, you can make relationships work and some people become lifelong partners. But there's a difference between staying with someone that you love, who you know isn't the one and living your life with someone you feel like you've known in a previous life. I know that if I had stayed with previous partners who I loved, I would not be completely happy and I would feel that something was missing. I didn't want love to be the reason I was unhappy. I knew that someone was waiting out there for me. It's just ironic that I was searching everywhere, and she was right before my eyes.

Love is something that we all want. There are different versions of love in the world, but ultimately it is all the same thing. Many of us don't think about the love we should show towards nature, animals, and the Universe. We tend to fixate on the idea that love must only be truly felt in a relationship. The key to feeling deep love in a relationship is initially falling in love with yourself. We often hear terms such as, "he loves himself so much" in a negative way, which is usually due to over confidence and living from ego, rather than from an actual deep love and appreciation for yourself.

To truly love yourself equals freedom. When you love yourself, your relationships will be so different. You will see the world in a more positive light and your insecurities will disappear. You need to look after your mind, body and spirit and be careful of who you let into your world. Your life is a precious gift, and you are full of unlimited potential. The following points will hopefully help you realise that you deserve the best, in all areas of your life. I also hope that they help you love yourself a little more, which will ultimately help you attract more love into your life.

Don't beat yourself up / Don't compare yourself to others

I've written articles about the power of social media, TV, film and magazines and how it can affect our mental health. Often, we look at others and start comparing ourselves. We want the bigger house, nicer clothes, more money, a more powerful job, and a "beautiful" partner, because to some people this defines success. You are uniquely beautiful, and you have your own journey. It's certainly good to have role models, but you need to be your own role model too. If you start comparing yourself to others and wanting to be like them, then you are putting too much pressure on yourself to be someone you are not. You need to be you and no other imitation. Don't beat yourself up too much about the small things. There are certain things in this life that you can't really do anything about. I'm 6ft 5 and there's nothing I can do about that. There were points in my life that I felt really out of place, because of my height. I learned to accept who I am and be proud of how tall I am and ignore what others said. It becomes very empowering when you start to release the need to please.

Exercise

We always hear how important exercise is and for some people the more we hear it, the less we want to do it. It's too easy to be lazy. Exercise doesn't have to be signing up to the gym and wanting to look like a god or a goddess. Just going for a walk is enough to start feeling better. Fresh air is so important, and it gives you time to listen to some music or get your head clear. The more you do it, the more you'll want to keep it up. Starting can be the hardest thing, but as soon as you do, you'll feel better. When you start to feel better, you will feel more confident. Confidence can open doors and opportunities for you.

Appreciate your body

You have a beautiful body! I love the fact that each person is so different. I love that we come in different shapes and sizes. It's what makes us unique. Some people find it hard to take a compliment. If you are one of those people, you must remember that you are truly beautiful. Once you get to a point of complete acceptance for who you are, you won't care what others think of you. I'm not going to get you to say affirmations in front of a mirror, but the shell that you call your body is yours and nobody else's. Look after it and appreciate it. It honestly doesn't matter what others think of you. Find something that you love about your body and be grateful.

Eat well

Don't eat too much junk food and drink plenty of water. Our society has made it too easy to order takeaways, eat on the go and not appreciate good, healthy food. I'm not saying to you that you shouldn't ever eat fast food. I believe that everything in moderation is fine, as long as you do exercise. You are in control of your body, and it is nobody else's responsibility. Eat a good range of fruit and vegetables and drink lots of water, as this has so many health benefits. It can reduce stress and anxiety, plus it can help you look better. If you pump yourself full of rubbish, you can block the universal flow.

Sleep

Many of us don't sleep enough. You can't function properly

without getting enough sleep. Maybe get a sleep app to see how long you are sleeping. If you are staying up later to watch TV or simply wasting time on social media, then put your phone down and get some rest. You will feel far better in the morning with an extra hour's sleep.

Use your time wisely

Time is precious. Do things in your life that excite you and do all the things that you've always wanted to do, because it will bring you a lot of joy. I understand that things can cost money. If you are in a tricky financial position, try and work out a system where you can save some money and spend some on personal experiences. It's a nice feeling when you look forward to something. Don't waste time dreaming about going somewhere. Put steps into place to actually make it happen. Spend your time with good people and positive people. It's not healthy if you are around toxic people who bring you down. Spend your time with people who bring the best out in you. Are you going to be around "drainers", who are going to drain your energy? Or are you going to surround yourself with "radiators", which are people who radiate love and kindness? Take ownership of your time.

Forgiveness / Let go

It can be so hard to forgive when someone has hurt you deeply. People can say that you need to "let go" and "move on", but it can be a really difficult thing to do, especially as most of the time we don't know how to move on or let go. Learn how to forgive yourself and others. If you hold onto negative emotions, it will stay with you all of your life and it can have an impact on your relationships and well-being. When you learn to forgive, any cloud hanging over your head will soon disappear. Once that cloud has lifted, you will be able to see clearer.

Take pride in your appearance

I love watching Queer Eye with my wife and I love how the Fab Five can help people feel better about themselves. Often this can come from taking more pride in your appearance. You can feel so much more confident and happier if you wear something nice. I'm not saying that you need to wear a suit every day, but you'll definitely feel better if you are inspired when you look in the wardrobe. Treat yourself to something that makes you feel good. Get your hair cut and buy some nice smelling perfume / aftershave. I can pretty much guarantee that you'll feel better. It feels good when you look good. You don't need to be vain, but it's okay to want to look good. It helps build confidence. I'm not saying that you should be someone you're not, but be the best version of yourself.

Make a vision board

I started making vision boards when I was in my late teens. They're really good to help you focus on what you want in life. It doesn't just have to be materialistic possessions. If you want more love and happiness in your life, then find an image that represents that. Fill the board with things that make you happy and all the things that you dream about. Look at it every day, visualise and imagine it as being yours already. You deserve all those things and more. Vision boards won't bring you results on their own, but they are a good prompt to remind you of your goals and to get into a place of "feeling" what you want.

Believe that you deserve the best from relationships and work

We all deserve to feel valued, and we all deserve to have a feeling of fulfilment from both work and relationships. If something doesn't feel right, it's because it isn't right! It's your responsibility to take action and sort it out. Nobody else is in control of your life other than you. I know it's not as easy as just quitting your job right now and then the perfect one just falling into your lap. However, do little things to move towards something that you really want to do. It's the same for relationships. If you are not happy, then change things. Don't let anyone take your power. Believe me, I know it's not easy to just "change things". I do however understand what it feels like to know in your heart that something isn't right. When I decided to change, it opened up some amazing relationships. You are not stuck where you are. You have a decision. Don't be afraid.

Get rid of negativity

There's no room for negativity in your life. A life full of love outshines any negativity. It's easy to get caught up in gossip and negative chat, especially when you're at work. Often, half the time, things are not as bad as they seem, it's just that the negativity pulls you down. As I mentioned earlier; Don't surround yourself with "drainers," you deserve to be around "radiators" who radiate happiness and bring out the best version of yourself.

Alone time

Often, we are too wrapped up in everyone else's lives, we struggle to be silent and alone. It's such a huge part of the healing process and understanding who you really are. Don't be afraid to embrace the silence and don't be afraid of your own company. If you are happy in your own company, then you won't look to others to fill the void. Being comfortable on your own is so important. Make sure you leave your phone alone and avoid reaching out on social media for a while. If you don't like your own company, how can you expect others to enjoy your company?

This is not a definitive list, but they are certainly things that helped me on my journey to self-discovery and appreciation. Remember that we are all different and we all experience life in our own way. What works for one person, doesn't necessarily work for someone else. Even if you embrace just two or three of these points, I guarantee that you will manage to get to a place of achieving more self-love.

We've heard it all before. Follow these steps and you will have a happy fulfilling relationship. The truth is, I think many people have experienced being in a relationship and had a feeling deep down that they shouldn't be in it. Maybe you are still in that relationship now, but don't know what to do. I know that I have felt that way many times. I learned a lot from each relationship and now I feel so blessed to have found my soul mate, but it wasn't an easy journey. The next ten steps are things that definitely work for me, and I hope that some of the points resonate with you. Please remember that this is just my experience. We all have different outlooks on life and different expectations in a relationship. It's important to work at having a harmonious relationship, with mutual love and respect.

Time

We are so guilty of saying "I don't have time for that". Whether it's going to the gym, taking up a hobby or spending time with our loved one. When we are in a relationship for a while, it's easy to just feel comfortable and get in a rut. It's crucial that you take time to appreciate each other. Look into each other's eyes, kiss, hug, and talk. Don't spend an hour on your phone at night just "being in each other's company." Use that time to remember why you fell in love and appreciate all the small things. If you are hugely busy, then book in a date night. It doesn't have to be every week. Maybe do it once a month and it can be something that you can both look forward to. If money is an issue, you can have a date night at home. Cook a nice meal, buy some wine, and watch a film together. Be in each other's company properly and be in the moment.

Honesty

Honesty is the key in any relationship, but you must remember to also be honest with yourself. It's a horrible thing when you struggle to admit to yourself that you just don't feel the same way anymore. So sometimes we continue perusing the relationship because we don't want to hurt the other person and we think we can't deal with the heartache. The brutal truth is that the sooner you realise and act on it, the better. Speaking from experience, I learned that it was far better to end a relationship that I honestly didn't want to be in, than keep pushing forward trying to make it work. In the end, everyone ended up a lot happier. The issue is we think short term and we don't want to be the person to open the can of worms. But you owe it to yourself and to the other person. Ultimately, we all want to be happy.

Friendship

At the end of the day, you both need to be the best of friends. A sustainable relationship simply can't last based on sex and lust. In my opinion, if you want to spend your life with someone, you must love their company. My wife is my best buddy. We make each other laugh, we play video games, go cycling, meditate, cook and we have even worked in the same place. We still have our own identity, but we just love each other's company and things are always better when we're together. I think it's because we were great friends before we started going out. When you get married and have children, things inevitably change. You won't have as much sex; you'll be tired and stressed, so you need to know that you can rely on your best mate to be by your side with no pressures.

Communication

It's hard enough understanding your own feelings sometimes, let alone trying to understand how someone else is feeling. Many relationships break down because they don't communicate how they feel about certain things. This could be stress from work, anger we hold from previous relationships, or anything else that's playing on our mind. You need to talk to each other. We all know that mental health is on the rise and talking to someone can be a simple way to help. This is why it's so important in a relationship. Some people are suffering in silence. If you can't talk to your partner, who can you talk to? As much as talking is important, it's just as important to listen. For those of you who are quite stubborn in your nature, try to understand how your partner is feeling, even if you don't like or understand it. Listen properly and give them time to explain and communicate. Don't tell lies. Do you like it when someone lies to you? Honesty can be difficult, but it's necessary.

Love

Often people get love and lust confused. They see someone who they think they have fallen in love with. Maybe they call it, "love at first sight." However, more often than not they have "fallen in lust." What happens is that over time, they emotionally hold onto that person thinking that they love them. They are afraid of letting them go, or they are afraid that they may cheat. This can often lead to obsession and possessive behaviour. True love doesn't require obsession or possession. In my experience, true love is easy. It just flows like a river. Of course there will be times when the river is a bit bumpy and there may be troubled waters, but it shouldn't be a fight and if you are a team, you get through the bumps easier.

Sex

Of course, sex is a massively important part of a relationship, but it shouldn't be based on sex alone. Sex is the most intimate, spiritual, powerful, and meaningful thing that you can do with someone. Often we throw it around as a meaningless act and we don't appreciate the emotional and spiritual attachment that can go with it. Some people are very self-conscious. Trusting to be naked with someone is a huge deal. Each person has different views on sex and that's fine. You need to be able to communicate your feelings about sex and be open and honest. Don't put pressure on having sex. It needs to happen naturally. As you get deeper into a relationship you may have less of it, but again, you need to keep talking. You can't be angry with your partner if they are not in the mood. Respect is important.

Laughter

If you and your partner can't laugh together then that sucks. Hopefully you want a relationship that can last a lifetime, if so, laughter is one of the things you need to share daily. Sometimes we say things like, "my partner makes me so happy." In all honesty, you can't give that power to someone else. You need to be happy before you enter a relationship. Others can add to it, but you need to be happy yourself. If you can laugh with your partner daily, then you are on to a winner. Laughter is the best medicine and it's infectious. Do something together each day that will make you both laugh.

Respect

Respect each other's mind, body, thoughts, decisions and wishes. I respect my wife so much and she respects me and all of my quirks. I have a lot of hobbies and she respects the fact that these are important things in my life. You shouldn't ever want to change someone. Respect who they are and what they believe in. Be respectful for their space and if they need time to be on their own, then that's okay.

Teamwork

You are a team. You have to do your part and your partner has to do their part. Use your initiative. If the house looks like a bombsite, then don't wait for your partner to ask you to tidy up. You're a grown up! I believe that everything should be a team effort around the house. As a team, my wife and I do the laundry, tidy the house, make the bed, wash the car, clean dog poo from the garden and all of the other mundane jobs. We don't have "specific jobs" we just get on with it as a team. You are both responsible. If one person feels they are doing all of the work, it can cause an imbalance which over time, can cause issues.

Trust

If you can't trust your partner, then I think you shouldn't be in the relationship. I have had issues in the past with trust and the feelings just kept eating away at me. I tried so hard to trust, but there was a heavy feeling that I was carrying around and it made me become someone who I didn't want to be. Trust works both ways though. I despise lying and being lied to, no matter how small it is. Never make a promise that you can't keep. Lying will break a relationship, cause insecurities, and potentially lead onto worse things. It can be hard to trust, so you both need to build it with all of the steps I have spoken about.

I understand that each person and each relationship is different. I'm not trying to tell you that we should all be the same. These points are the simple fundamental rules of my marriage, which work for us. You don't want to be in a relationship for the sake of being in a relationship, that will do neither of you any favours. You deserve to be in a happy fulfilling relationship without any compromise. You shouldn't have to say, "my partner is awesome… but." Honestly at times, I wondered if I ever believed that such relationships actually existed. It turns out that after a lot of dating and heartache… It absolutely does and you can find it too.

ACTION POINTS

- Be comfortable in your own company
- Let go
- Respect every relationship
- Don't just settle. You deserve the best

CHAPTER THREE
LIFE IS A GAME

I often think of life as a game. Some people win and some people lose. Some people don't realise that they are winning, even when they are! Imagine life as a game of Monopoly. Some get lucky and collect lots of money, get all the houses and win the beauty competitions. Then there's the other end of the scale. People struggling to buy the property they want, constantly paying bills they don't have enough money for. They feel bad when they land on someone else's property and have to pay rent. There are also people in the middle, who play the game but are not necessarily winners or losers. They just get on with it. They don't make "big bucks", but they are content and happy to be just playing the game. Think about your life. Which one are you? Are you the one struggling? Are you the one who is content with just playing? Or are you the one winning the game? Are you the one who starts the game with the intent to beat everyone, grab all the money, bankrupt everyone and laugh about their misfortune, while you are stacking in the cash? We all have a different approach to life and that's what makes it so interesting. One thing that we all have in common is that the Law of Attraction and Synchronicity are working with us, but most of the time we are completely unaware.

We can apply the Monopoly analogy to our own life. I ask you to consider which way you are playing your actual game of life. Where is your focus? Where is your energy going? Have you ever set out to play Monopoly with the mindset to screw everyone over to win and then lost dramatically? It's a win at all cost attitude and although it's important to put everything you have into a goal, it's important to get to the root of why we actually want to achieve this goal in the first place. Is it a healthy goal? Is it benefiting you, your family, and the world? A bit of healthy competition is fine, but I'm not a believer at win at all costs and here's why.

We don't always know the bigger picture

Sometimes we set off to achieve a specific goal, but we have no idea how we are going to get there. We think that life is going to pan out a certain way and then something completely out the blue knocks us off course and throws us a massive curve ball. Sometimes these moments are brilliant, but sometimes they can be extremely difficult challenges. One thing is for sure though. Whatever it is that happened, happened for a reason. It's so hard to believe that sometimes, but it's true. I've been through some pretty dark times. In the moment, I had no idea why my world was falling down around me. It was only later when I looked back that everything made sense. If it wasn't for those things happening, I would not have learned some valuable lessons and it wouldn't have led me to where I am now.

Sometimes we act more from ego

Some people want the money, the house, the car, the status, and the power. They want to win at all costs to prove to people that they have won. To show everyone how successful they are. They want to be on top and stay on top. You don't have to win at everything, be mega rich, have a huge house and break all the records to be happy. I live a pretty ordinary life, but I'm really happy and my family is happy. We go on holiday; we have a car and treat ourselves to things when we want. I certainly have goals, but in the recent years I have re-evaluated why I chose specific goals. Honestly, some of the things I wanted were more ego driven than anything. I wanted to feel loved, respected, powerful, and important. If this is your main focus, then it's not necessarily a good starting point, as it is not coming from a place of love. It's coming from a place of fear and lack.

It loses its joy

Achieving your goals should be fun and you should feel a sense of joy every time you do something towards achieving them. When it becomes a competition against other people, you are losing the sight of what is important. When it becomes a struggle and stress and anxiety kick in, then you need to stop and pause and ask yourself if this is really what you want. I'm not saying that you should give up on your goals, but I'm a firm believer of enjoying your work. If you are not enjoying it, then why are you doing it? Sometimes when we act on our instincts and follow our joy, things that we need fall into our lap. On the other hand, sometimes we feel as though we are knocking our heads against a brick wall, jumping lots of hurdles and reaching our goal is like a constant obstacle course. Deep down we need to listen to what our heart is telling us. I have definitely chased dreams that deep down I know were driven from ego, rather than from love. What I discovered was that the dreams I chased from the heart were a lot easier to make a reality than those driven by ego.

You're not letting the Universe help you

You're not trusting. You're like a fish swimming down river going from bank to bank getting stressed and determined to get to the end, not realising that the flow is there helping you, if you allow it to. Sometimes we have to let go and just go with the flow. We get impatient. We are so used to living in a "now society" that we forget that it's okay to wait for a little while. I think back to the days of VHS and Cassette Tapes. I had to listen to the radio and wait for my favourite songs to come on. At Christmas I looked through the list of movies that will be aired and waited patiently for them to play. We now have everything with a click of a button. Music, just type it into Spotify. Movies, just download it on iTunes or watch in on any of the streaming platforms. The latest gadget, just order it on Amazon. Fast food, just order it on your Just Eat app. You must trust in the Universe.

Enjoy the game. You are not here to suffer. You were made from love, and you ARE love. It's this love that connects us all. It's this love that can clear our limitations and bring our dreams into reality. How are you going to play your game of life?

ACTION POINTS

- Focus your energy into abundance
- You don't need to know the answers. Have faith
- Allow the Universe to deliver

CHAPTER FOUR
TIME IS JUST AN ILLUSION

"The relativity of space and of time is a startling conclusion. I have known about it for more than twenty-five years, but even so, whenever I quietly sit and think it through, I am amazed. From the well-worn statement that the speed of light is constant, we conclude that space and time are in the eye of the beholder. Each of us carries our own clock, our own monitor of the passage of time. Each clock is equally precise, yet when we move relative to one another, these clocks do not agree. They fall out of synchronization; they measure different amounts of elapsed time between two chosen events." – Brian Greene – The Fabric of the Cosmos

Time isn't real. Time is a thing that we use on this planet to help us stay organised and to give us routine. I'm a big believer of organisation and routine, but when we look at what's happening at the atomic level and the nature of the Universe, it's anything but organised. I was introduced to a book called Fabric of the Cosmos, by Brian Greene. There is also a four-part documentary based on this book and its mind blowing. I highly suggest watching or reading it. Next time you are on an airplane, look out of the window and watch the millions of people living out their daily life, driving to work, going for a run, walking their dog and so on. It's chaos. It is also completely unpredictable. But we try and make it more predictable by using time. We don't like it when things get in our way. We get stressed on a Monday morning when we think we are on time, and we walk outside to get into the car and realise that the car windows are covered in ice. Now we'll be late for work because we need to stand there waiting for the demisters to warm up while we scrape off the ice with an old CD case. We are constantly chasing time. But time doesn't exist and it's irrelevant to the Universe. There are theories that everything that has happened or will happen is actually all happening at once! Maybe the Universe wanted something to get in your way today. Maybe it was a sign which you are not seeing due to the fixation of time.

We can't really comprehend this idea of no time because it rules our life. Why is this relevant to the Law of Attraction and Synchronicity? Well, if the Universe is not affected by time in the same way we are, then the only thing putting limitations on what we attract is ourselves. We expect things to take time. We expect obstacles and because we want it NOW, we are not trusting that the Universe can actually give it to us now. So, what happens? It takes longer for us to manifest it into our lives. My ex-fiancé actually introduced me to Fabric of the Cosmos and The Celestine Prophecy. Both of these books changed my life. Although we are no longer together, I see the synchronicities in our time together. It certainly wasn't the easiest time in my life, but I'm grateful and I know that it happened for a reason.

At times I have manifested things so quickly I can't quite believe it. Sometimes I've barely even tried, and things have just come to me. Reflecting on those times, I think it's due to the fact that it wasn't about ego. It wasn't about ME. It wasn't coming from a point of me thinking "I NEED this! I WANT it NOW!" For example, I decided to set up a Radio-Controlled car club at the school I teach at. I asked my Head of Department if he could give me £200 to buy a Tamiya Lunchbox kit car so that I could build it with a team of pupils. I put a poster up at school and I had 20 pupils sign up in one day. As amazed as I was, I thought that one car between 20 pupils wouldn't be enough. Without any expectation I put a post on the Tamiya Facebook group saying that I have a group of 20 kids excited to build a car and race it around the school playground. Because of that one comment, I had 6 cars donated to the school for free! One of my colleagues came into work one day with a box of vintage R/C cars and gave them to me. As I did a bit of research on the cars, I realised that they were extremely rare and worth a lot of money. They were all in pieces and had been sat in a box in a garage for 20 years or more. I sent a message to the guy that gave them to me to say that if I sold them, I'll get almost £400. We decided to sell the cars and split the money. My colleague got £200 for doing nothing and I got £200 to buy another car and spare parts.

I took inspired action setting up the R/C car club. It was something that I had a lot of joy doing in my childhood and I wanted to share that joy. I took inspired action by posting something on the Facebook group. I wasn't expecting anything, but I absolutely attracted 6 extra cars and £200 from the cars we sold. All of this came from a single idea. I could have quite easily not acted on it. But look at the good that's come from it. I have pupils who enjoy a new hobby, my colleague cleared some space in the garage and made £200. Some generous strangers did some good by donating to a school and we are all better off. It's amazing what we can do when we act on our intuition, follow our gut feelings, ask the Universe and let go. All I did was say to myself, "we need more cars for these kids to enjoy," then act on any guidance. The Universe delivered. Literally 2 days later.

Do you often say, "Time is precious" or "I don't have enough time?" We are mortal physical beings, but our spirit is immortal. Unfortunately, most of the time the mortal part of us takes over and convinces us that we don't have enough time. We catch ourselves saying, "I'm almost 40 years old. I'm getting so old." It's so frustrating to hear and I'm also guilty of it. I often say, "I can't do what I did when I was in my 20's" and when I hear myself say these words, I try to correct it. If this becomes a habit, I will start giving myself limiting beliefs that I can't do it. Subsequently, I will then have to clear these beliefs. It will just make the process of attracting that much harder! We convince ourselves that we don't have enough time and say, "time speeds up when you get older." People have asked me how I have time to draw my portraits, play in a band, write a book, teach full time and still be a good husband and father. I believe that if you really want to do something, you make time for it. My son goes to bed at 7:30pm and

I go to bed at 10:00pm. That gives me 2 and a half hours for me to write or draw. It's also my "mindfulness time". When I write, draw or play guitar, I am completely absorbed in what I am doing and it's my escapism. For some people, that would be watching a TV series or movie. For me though, I like to spend that time being creative in some way. If you say that you don't have time to do stretches or exercise. Why can't you do that while watching TV? I have to do daily stretches on my Erb's Palsy arm. I often do them before my son goes to bed while he is watching a cartoon. More often than not, he'll just jump on me and try to wrestle me, but I make it into a game!

What would you do if you have 2 and a half hours free today to do what you wanted? Would you waste the time? Would you use it wisely? Don't get me wrong. It's really important to take time to relax and to switch off, but if you want to do something enough, you find ways to make the time. Also, remember the importance of being in the "now." We are often focused so much on our goal, we are not in the present moment.

"But without a sense of time, how would we function in this world? There would be no goals to strive toward anymore. I wouldn't even know who I am, because my past makes me who I am today. I think time is something very precious, and we need to learn to use it wisely rather than waste it. Time isn't precious at all, because it is an illusion. What you perceive as precious is not time but the one point that is out of time: the Now. That is precious indeed. The more you are focused on time past and future the more you miss the Now, the most precious thing there is."
Eckhart Tolle – The Power of Now

Our mind conjures up pictures of the future and the past. The images that we have of the past are fragmented pictures, which are mostly inaccurate. We piece them together to create a memory. When we describe these images of the past, we forget all of the small details and what we are actually remembering are false images. Have you ever reminisced with an old friend and your stories are slightly different? This is because we have forgotten a lot of the details and we fill in the gaps. When we visualise the future, we use images we've learned from the past to create an image of what we want it to be. This is based on learned behaviour and limited beliefs, so we need to be careful what we visualise and imagine, as a lot of it will be based on a lie. If some of the memories you have are not very pleasant, we can slip into protective mode. We remember what we want to remember, rather than what actually happened.

The reason I'm talking about this is because we need to ensure we live in the moment as much as we can. This is the only "time" that we can be sure of. We are often distracted by our own goals! They take up a lot of head space and we fixate on making them happen. If you allow the Law of Attraction to do what it needs to do, then you can let go, trust, and know that whatever you want will manifest. You don't need to waste your time in your own head by being in the future or by trying to put all of the pieces of the puzzle together. Feel the ground beneath your feet, breathe in the air, appreciate everything that is around you, for this is the only time you really need to be concerned with.

ACTION POINTS

- Monitor your words. Re-phrase everyday sayings to make them positive
- Make time for the things you want to do
- Be in the moment

CHAPTER FIVE
TUNE INTO THE RIGHT FREQUENCY

"Your world, present and future, is directly and specifically affected by the signal that you are now transmitting. The personality that is You is really an eternal personality, but who you are right now, and what you are thinking right now, is causing a focusing of Energy that is very powerful. This Energy that you are focusing is the same Energy that creates worlds. And it is, in this very moment, creating your world." Esther and Jerry Hicks – Ask and it is given

Have you ever seen a game show where they do "Grab a grand"? The contenders go inside a plastic dome and then the game master puts in loads of money, the wind blows up and they have to grab as much as then can. Imagine people and everything on this planet like that. We are constantly trying to grab the money or the thing that we want, but we can never grab all we want. The more we try, the harder it becomes and we end up disappointed that we didn't grab enough.

Now, imagine that every pound note blowing around has an energy frequency. Visualise tuning your frequency to the same one as the pound notes. What will happen? Because you are now vibrating on the same frequency, you will attract it like a magnet. The pound notes in the plastic dome don't just represent money. They can be anything. They can be people, books, experiences, opportunities etc. My point is, amongst the chaos of the Universe, you can tune into the frequency of that thing you want. You can, to a certain extent allow things to come to you (like I did with the R/C cars) but there will always be a need to act.

A lot of the time people are happy to tune into the frequency and then wait for things to fall into their lap. One of the most important lessons I learned about manifesting, was in a book by Dr Joe Vitale called Attract Money Now. He says that you need to take "inspired action". These two words changed my life. I consider myself to be a really fortunate person. Ever since I was a boy I came up with crazy ideas. Whether that would be ideas for products, businesses, books, or TV show ideas. They would just come to me. Did I ever act on any of them? No, not really. Maybe to a certain extent I did, but I didn't follow them through to a point of making them a reality. If I did, who knows what I would be doing now. But I don't like to live in the "what if". I like to live in the "now" and the "what next". I still get random ideas come to me. I jot them down and if I feel really inspired, then I will act on it. I had the idea for this book on the way to work one day when I was listening to the Attract Money Now audiobook by Joe Vitale. The idea just came to me and as soon as I got into work, I purchased the domain www.ificanyoucanthebook.com and I was flooded with ideas. When we listen to or read inspiring books, it often opens the creative doors. We just need to make sure that we actually do something about it. I felt a deep feeling of excitement and joy thinking about writing this book. I wrote a short book in 2008 called One Mans' Thoughts. This was more of a therapeutic act for me, but I decided to go with the flow and just write what I was thinking. I don't necessarily think, or write the same as I did back then, but it was certainly a good experience for me. This time it feels different. So much has changed in my life since then. Throughout this book I talk about some of my darker times and my joyful times. As you are reading the stories, you should be able to work out what frequency I was on. Truth be told, it wasn't always on the correct one. But we can't expect to be perfectly tuned in 100 percent of the time. As I mentioned before, if it becomes hard work, then you are doing something wrong. Of course, we have bad times in life. Everybody goes through difficulties. My point is that we need to make sure that when those difficult times do arise, we shift our focus and get back onto the right frequency.

Everything is vibration. Your thoughts can vibrate on the same frequency as your desires. It just takes a little bit of practice to tune it in. Everything that we do or say is vibration and those vibrations ripple out into the Universe. With that in mind, you need to make sure that you monitor your thoughts and actions. I'd like to share an extract from The Law of Attraction by Esther and Jerry Hicks…

The Law of attraction is responsible for much that is obvious in your life experience. You have coined many phrases because of your partial understanding of this law. You say, "Birds of a feather flock together." You say, "The better it gets, the better it gets; and the worse it gets, the worse it gets." You say, "This day started out bad and ended up much, much worse." But even as you are saying these things, most of you do not truly understand how powerful the Law of Attraction really is. People are drawn together because of it. Every circumstance and event is a result of it... Thoughts that are vibrationally similar to one another are drawn magnetically to one another through the powerful Law of Attraction; people who feel a certain way are drawn to one another, magnetically, through this law; indeed, the very thoughts that you think are drawn one unto the other until what was once a very small or insignificant and not-so-powerful thought may, because of your focus upon it, grow to be very powerful.

Because of the Law of Attraction, each of you is like a powerful magnet, attracting unto you more of the way that you feel at any point in time. The Law of Attraction – Esther and Jerry Hicks

What I hope that you understand from this extract is what you think about vibrationally, you will bring into your life. If you are wanting to attract a new car, money or house, you must realise that those "things" have a vibrational energy. As do you. If you attract people who have the same beliefs as you, you can attract anything, as long as you are tuning into its frequency. It sounds easy when I say it like that, but you still need to make it happen. Can you learn to want without need? It's important to "welcome" things in your life, rather than "want" things in your life, as want comes from lack.

Have you ever walked into a room, and sensed the energy or tension? You can tell if someone has had an argument, as there is a certain "feeling" in the room. This is energy, frequency, vibration, or whatever you want to call it. It is a very real thing, and we give it to people or things without thinking. If you have ever visited Auschwitz, you will know exactly what I am talking about. It is impossible to visit without feeling the energy of the appalling evil that happened there. Our thoughts create actions and our actions resonate through the Universe. If you can learn to understand that every single thing on this planet is vibration, you will start to learn how to tune into that "thing" which you desire.

Several years ago, I met up with a close friend of mine. We went for dinner, and we talked for hours about spirituality, energy and meditation. This was all reasonably new to him and he was fascinated and wanted to understand more. I told him a story of a recent spiritual festival I attended…

I like to go where I am drawn to go. If I feel that I need to go somewhere, I will follow that instinct. I decided to attend a very low-key spiritual festival one weekend. I didn't really think too much of it. I decided to go, so I went. When I got there, I set up my tent and walked around to get a feel for the place. I noticed some people sitting on the floor and gathering in a circle. I was intrigued, so I walked over. We were in the middle of nowhere and you couldn't hear any hum of the roads or see any light pollution. It's always so nice to reconnect with mother nature. One of the guys asked me to sit in the circle. He said that we will be connecting with the Elves, Pixies, Fairies and Angels of this land. We are going to interact with them and ask them to help us on our quest. I'm a pretty open-minded person. I have angel cards and I certainly believe in a lot of things that some people would ridicule me for, but I had never "called in Elves, Pixies and Fairies". This seemed a little far out.

Nevertheless, I joined in and approached it with an open mind. We started with a meditation to ground us and to connect with the earth around us. Once we were peaceful and open the guy leading the session asked us to put our hand out. He said to ask for a fairy, elf, or pixie to jump up and sit on your hand. He said, "If you can't feel anything then ask them to stand by your side. Use you hand and move it up and down slowly until you can feel something. I put my hand out in front of me and in my head, I asked a fairy to sit on it. I had the strangest sensation. It felt like a feather had landed in the middle of my hand. Although I couldn't see anything, I knew something was there. I didn't know what it looked like, but I could feel it there, as real as anything. I could sense how big it was, so I used my other hand and lowered it slowly on top of the other. I stopped around 12 inches before my hands connected. My hand didn't want to move any more. There was something there. To some, this may sound utterly bonkers, but this was as real as me sitting here typing these words. After a while, he asked each of us to keep them in our hands and take it in turns to talk about our experiences. As we spoke one at a time, I realised that we all had similar experiences. I described mine to the group and everyone looked and said they could also sense the same thing by looking at my hand. Once we finished, I asked it to jump off my hand and, in an instant, I felt it leave. As I write these words, my hands feel full of energy, and I get the feeling that it is here beside me. It feels beautiful.

For around six years I studied Tai Chi. I absolutely loved it. I had a weekly two-hour lesson. During the first hour, we would do the slow meditative moves and in the second half we would do the martial arts form, which not all Tai Chi instructors teach. We would warm up by doing some Chi Gong, which was incredible. If you have never done it before, it's worth giving it a go. One of the exercises requires you to stand with your legs slightly bent and raise your hands palm up on your in breath and on your out breath, turn them over and lower them. After a while, on the out breath, you feel as though you have a balloon which you are trying to push under water. You can feel the energy and sense it with all of your being.

Often when I meditate, I have my hands in the prayer position. After a while, they take on a mind of their own. It used to happen when I attended a Reiki Share Group. My hands and arms just unconsciously move. I don't intentionally do it, it's like an energy is taking over. More often than not, my hands will end up together and I feel a ball of energy in my hands. If they don't do this, I can sense a ball in each hand. I can't push my hands together, it feels as real as having a physical ball there.

I explained this to my friend over dinner and he was really intrigued. As I was talking, I could sense that my hands were warming up and that there was energy there. I put my hand out and I could feel something there. I asked him to lower his hand on top of mine and stop when he felt something. He raised his hand and slowly started lowering it. After a few seconds, his eyes lit up and just stared at me.

"Oh my God!" he said in amazement. He had never experienced

anything like this before.

"Can you feel it?" I asked him.

"I can't push my hand down any further," he replied.

"There you go. Energy and vibration is a real thing. What you think about, you can bring into your life. This is an example of focusing your energy."

When I was a child, my mum wanted to show me the power of thought and how we can focus our energy. She asked me to link my thumb and index finger together to make a chain. She told me that she was going to try and pull them apart, but to try and resist. I put all of my might into it, but she managed to succeed in pulling them apart. She asked me to close my eyes and focus on the fingers not breaking their connection. Take some deep breaths and imagine energy flowing down through my arms and into my fingers. After a few moments, she tried again. She tried with all her might, but as I stood there, I effortlessly kept my fingers linked together, by focusing my thoughts and energy. I tried this in a school assembly last year, as I was talking about the power of our thoughts and concentration. Many pupils came up to me in disbelief. They couldn't believe it.

The reason I'm telling you this is because your energy is a real thing. You can use it for your advantage and to help those around you. You can use it to connect with the spirit world and to get in alignment with the things that you want. You must do this with an open mind and for the greater good. Work from love, peace and a place of abundance. You are a magnet. You can become an even stronger magnet when you start to learn how to use your powers. We see people use the power of focus and concentration on the sports field or doing a 100-metre sprint. You may have heard people refer to it as being "in the zone." They are visualising something so intently, that they are living each moment of the race. When you visualise, you must do the same thing. When you pray and you feel everything that you are asking for, you feel it with every part of your body. This is how you tune into the frequency of the things you want. Visualisation is not enough on its own. It needs to come from feeling. As you build that energy inside of you, you are connecting and getting into the flow of the Universe and when you do step into the flow, it delivers all that you need.

ACTION POINTS

- Tune into the flow of the Universe
- Write down ideas that you have and act on them
- Trust in the divine

CHAPTER SIX
THE MUSIC DREAM

I started playing the drums at a young age as a form of exercise for my Erb's Palsy (I will talk more about Erb's Palsy in Chapter Seven). I was told I'd never be able to play guitar due to very limited movement that I have in my arm and fingers. Despite this, I asked for a guitar for my 18th birthday. I knew that I wanted to play the guitar, but I didn't really know how to. We had an old guitar around the house and one day I picked it up. I naturally started playing it upside down. It turns out that I could play left-handed! My right hand could play the chords and my Erb's Palsy arm could do the strumming and fingerpicking. I always dreamt of being on stage. I loved being in the school shows and standing with the school choir, singing my heart out. I decided I wanted to record an album and then send it off to record companies and radio stations. The hope was that someone may like it and subsequently help me make it into the world of music to fulfil my dreams.

My friend Trystan (now my closest and oldest friend) had set his spare bedroom up into a recording studio and over the course of a year we put an album together. I wrote all of the songs, and he used his amazing skills to make them sound as good as they could do. Bearing in mind I had only been playing guitar for a year or two at the most, I felt pretty good about these songs. Some of my friends at the time didn't really take me seriously. When we went out for drinks, they would mock me and be really critical. It's important to listen to advice and proper feedback from your friends and family, but their mocking made me feel rubbish. Subconsciously, I think this has stuck with me. Because I never cleared this negativity, I had limited "success" in the music world. I know I can clear these beliefs and one day I will, but for now my focus is on other things.

As I started to play more gigs, I became more confident. My song writing also improved. I decided to put together a quality album and really focus on every detail. Fortunately, Trystan believed in my songs. He worked with me each step of the way and helped bring out the best in me. This is what good friends should do. It's safe to say that I no longer associate with those people who mocked me. I don't have time for negativity in my life. Trystan played a few of the new songs to his boss and he said it'd be great to record a full orchestra, to really capture the emotion of the songs. I thought this was a great idea. I was spending a lot of money on this album, assuming that it would be a success. Trystan often uses Abbey Road Recording Studios, so we were initially looking at booking a session there, but it wasn't available when we wanted it. Instead, we used Angel Record Studios, which was the closest alternative. It was an incredible experience. To be amongst the powerful orchestra playing music that I had written bought tears to my eyes. I couldn't quite believe where I was. After a few more months of mixings and mastering I had a finished product. A twelve-track album called Inner Strength. I had 1000 CDs made up, found a distributor to get my music on all of the major download and streaming platforms and then… I gave up.

Something happened inside of me. I played a few acoustic gigs and hosted some open mic nights. I played a lot of my new songs, which people seemed to enjoy. I would play cover songs like Wonderwall by Oasis and the crowd would go mad, sing along and then shout out similar requests. The more gigs I played the more frustrated I became. No one was really buying my CDs. I had this album that I was really proud of, which cost me a lot of money to make, sat there in their boxes. I was saying to myself that people don't want to pay money for music, they want it for free. People only want to listen to me play cover songs and sing along while they are drunk. I'm playing my songs alone with an acoustic guitar, this doesn't even represent the songs on the album with a full band and orchestra. I'm so frustrated. I became more disillusioned with the idea and stopped gigging. I sent CDs off to radio stations and record companies but to no avail. One company guaranteed air play, so I gave them £1000 for them to push my music, as they promised results. I still don't know to this day if they did what they said they would. I felt a bit cheated and frustrated by it all. I kept reading articles about how only younger artists are likely to make it in the music industry and that you only have one shot and if you miss that shot, it's game over. What was the point? The dream had gone. I'd wasted my time and money.

I have carried those beliefs around with me since I released that album in 2009. But what should I have done? I should have played the cover songs and enjoyed playing them. I should have been grateful to have had the opportunities to play live and for the CDs that I DID sell. Rather than moaning and focusing on the negatives, I should have been grateful for these experiences. It would have opened more opportunities and I would have met more people. Instead, I got frustrated and gave up. I began that journey hoping that a music career would just fall into my lap. What we focus and act on, we bring into our lives. I was focused on not many CD sales and guess what? Yep, you got it. I didn't sell many CDs.

I'm very proud of that album and in many ways, I do consider it a success. But how do we measure success? Success is relative to the bar that we set and limitations that we put on ourselves. Being successful doesn't mean you have to be rich and famous. The point of this story is that I took inspired action. I made an album (and several since, including two EPs with my band – I didn't truly give up). That album created the opportunity to work with a 16-piece orchestra, one that opened up gig opportunities and many other doors, which at the time I had no idea opened.

Reflecting on my dream to be a musician I realised that my motivation was to be admired and loved. I wanted to walk on the stage and for everyone to sing my songs back at me. I wanted that power. To have a huge crowd sing your song back at you is the ultimate songwriter's dream. My dream was coming from ego, and this was the biggest issue. I wanted it because it looked fun and easy. I wanted to sign autographs, go on TV shows, and mix with the rich and famous. My goal was shallow, and my focus was completely on the wrong thing. I wasn't listening to divine inspiration. I was listening to ego. My dreams have changed somewhat now. So many self-help books talk about achieving your wildest dreams. They can absolutely work, but for me, deep down, I felt that I was destined for something else.

When I became a teacher, my life made a lot more sense. It just felt right. I used all of my experiences gigging, recording, and writing to start a club with the kids called School of Rock. Although it had similarities to the movie, we met once a week to make some noise. I helped the pupils write songs, play the instruments, and show them what it means to be in a band. Each year we went to a recording studio to record the songs that we had written throughout the year. We put on several concerts, and it was a joyous thing to do. I don't believe that I wasted my time gigging and releasing music. It allowed me to give the pupils who came to the club an opportunity to do something they may never have otherwise done. It gave them fond memories and for some, a bit of experience to help them succeed as musicians. My original goal was ego driven and coming from a need of love and appreciation from others. Although I haven't yet achieved my original vision of that goal, I wasn't to foresee the impact it would have upon my pupils. We don't know how things are meant to unfold for us and in many ways, it is good not to know. We don't know how our actions and decisions will affect those around us. This is why it's important to act on divine inspiration. It may not be you who will be benefiting from it. Maybe you are being given an idea which you think is for you, but it's actually for someone else. The universe works in mysterious ways and who are we to argue?

ACTION POINTS

- Understand that there is a bigger picture, and we don't need to know 'how'
- Let the Universe guide you
- Set goals from inspiration, not from ego

CHAPTER SEVEN
OPEN THE DOORS

Sometimes we do things, but we don't realise at the time where it will lead us. We are looking for doors to open up for us. Often, we are too focused on a specific door; we don't see the others. For example, in the previous chapter I wanted a door to open right into a record company office. I wasn't looking for any other doors. I didn't SEE any other doors. Sometimes these doors open for us in a different room, we just need to get to that specific room! Sometimes the actions we take lead us somewhere completely different and that's more than okay. So many good things have come to me from making that album. I never got signed by a record label, but if I hadn't made that album. I wouldn't be writing this book and I wouldn't have met some incredible people. Do I consider the album to be a success? Hell yes, I do.

One of the first doors that opened for me was a door that was well and truly shut. I hadn't even thought about opening it and I'm not sure

I even wanted to open it. I was born with Erb's Palsy, which is also known as Brachial Plexus Injury. I was a big baby (almost 11lbs) and on my way into this world I got stuck. Due to the complications, I ended up being pulled by my arm and having nerves torn, leaving me with a paralysed left arm. (I could write a whole book on living with Erb's Palsy, but I'll leave that for another time.)

I had daily physiotherapy and over time I regained around 60% movement. Growing up I didn't really feel too different. I was very much in my own little world and I was always daydreaming. One of the schools I attended was particularly difficult for me. Some of the kids I hung around with were pretty mean to me. They noticed I was a little different and started calling me 'Paralysed Parsons' and imitating the way my arm and wrist hung. As a child, we don't realise the impact that we have on others and how our actions can stay with someone for the rest of their life. They also bullied me because of my glasses and the way I spoke. I was just a normal guy in a posh prep school and because I didn't look or sound like them, or have as much money as them, I was an easy target. To this day I'm still not 100% confident wearing glasses, despite my wife telling me I actually look better when I wear them. There are definitely things I still need to work on, but this is an ongoing thing for all of us. It can be hard to clear limiting beliefs and negative subconscious thoughts about ourselves. In many ways, this is the hardest part of the manifestation process. I will talk more about self-love, acceptance, and appreciation in Chapter Nineteen, but some of the things I have manifested have come through the love of the project that I'm doing, rather than the love of myself. An example of that was the Radio-Controlled cars that I attracted for the school club.

When I try to manifest something for myself, I find it harder because I still haven't got to a point where I truly love and accept everything about myself. Sadly, I think this is due to the influence of others in my past. Forgiveness is so powerful, but a very difficult thing to do. It's easy to blame others for how you feel and to look to others to make you happy, but this is not empowerment. Like many people, my beliefs were formed at a young age, and they have stuck with me for a long time. Clearing these old beliefs can be hard to do, but it can be done with the right techniques. How do you truly love yourself when, as a child you were criticized and bullied? You are like a sponge when you are a child. You believe everything and you are easily influenced. Re-learning that stuff is very difficult, but with patience and practice you can get there.

I got tired of being picked on at school. I couldn't understand why they were doing this to me. Why were they being so mean to me? I hadn't done anything to deserve this. I couldn't help the fact my arm wasn't normal. I couldn't help the fact I had to wear glasses. Looking back, I didn't do myself any favours. As I mentioned earlier, I was a daydreamer. I was very naïve and didn't know any better. I went to a prep school where many of the other children were boarders. Every now and then I would stay over too. I LOVED the Lion King movie, and I had an amazing Lion King duvet. I loved it so much (in fact, I still have it. It's on my son's bed as I write this). Safe to say, owning this duvet was a golden opportunity for the kids at school to bully me.

They made me feel awful and I even stopped watching the film due to the things they said. Their actions always seemed so far away from anything that I would do and I couldn't comprehend why they even thought what they did, let alone act on it. My classroom was on the top floor of the school and my so-called friends would take my golf bag and empty the clubs out of the window into the bush below. They would often do this just before we went for golf lessons. Similarly, before a teacher would walk in to teach, they were known to take my pencil case and throw it out of the window so that I had no equipment for the lesson. I was new to this type of behaviour as my previous schools were very different. Was this how I was supposed to behave too?

During the last year at that school, I went to a birthday party in Yorkshire. One of the girls lived up north and her parents hired a coach for all of us to go and camp in their garden, have a disco, and celebrate her 13th birthday. For some reason that night, I decided that I'd had enough. One of my so-called friends asked the DJ to play 'In the Jungle' from The Lion King and dedicate it to Matt 'Simba' Parsons. Everyone turned and looked at me and laughed. I was so embarrassed and angry. What have I done to deserve this? In that moment, rather than reacting and causing a laugh which is normally what happened. I laughed! Everyone looked shocked. This was not the normal reaction from them. If I reacted negatively, they did it even more. In that moment I learned how to laugh it off. They never did it again. Maybe I used to take myself too seriously, I don't know. I now realise that I was attracting more of the negativity to me. I was letting them take my energy. The more I focused on it, the more they did it. As I'm writing this, I'm telling you that, "they made me feel awful". Now, although what they were doing wasn't very nice, I wasn't in control of my own power. My mum used to say to me, "use silent power." At the time I didn't really understand what it meant, but now it's very clear.

That night, I had the first conscious spiritual experience of my life. It was around midnight and people were going to sleep. I didn't want to share a tent with anyone. I wasn't tired and I wanted to be by myself. I decided to go for a walk around the vast grounds. It was a warm summer night. The long grass was up to my waist and there was a path that had been cut out for people to walk through. The sky was full of stars and the local village was twinkling in the distance as I looked down from the top of the hill. I laid down in the grass and stared up at the stars in awe as the warm breeze covered me. I felt like the Universe had swallowed me up and I was drifting in a sea of stars and planets. I don't remember how long I was there for, but it felt like a lifetime. That was the moment I realised that the Universe was on my side and that I was an important part of it. I couldn't put it into those words, but it was a feeling that I had in every part of my being. I was here for a reason. I was born into this experience and into this time for a purpose. What that purpose is, I still don't exactly know. But I still have that feeling. We are all here for a reason and our lives entwine with others. We absolutely effect the things around us and our purpose, no matter how small, has a great effect on the Universe and those around us.

When I think back to the moment on the dancefloor when the DJ played that song. I chose to change the way I reacted. My actions changed my reality. I was so fed up with trying to work out WHY these people were being so horrible to me. What I didn't realise was I bringing more of it to me through the Law of Attraction. The more I was focusing on the WHY and the way it made me FEEL, the more it was coming into my life. As soon as I changed the way I thought about it and laughed, it immediately changed my outer world.

A similar thing happened when I was at university. I studied Fine Art and while I was there, George Bush was President of the United States of America. I was so happy to have the freedom to paint what I wanted, so I experimented a lot with the creativity. This was just after 9/11 and there was a lot of theories about Bush, and he was in the news a lot. There were videos and articles online containing many of the silly things that he has said. I was frustrated and angry at all of the fighting that was taking place around the world. I was angry that people kill in the name of God. I decided to focus my artwork on this topic. The more art I was producing, the more depressed and angrier I got. I was miserable. My art tutor wasn't giving me good grades and then I was getting even more angry and fed up. Why wasn't anyone taking this seriously? Why can't I change the world? Why are people fighting? Why are we killing each other? Why is the president saying God told him to go to war? Aggghhhh.

I hadn't realised that the rest of my life was also being affected by my anger and frustration. My spotlight of attention was constantly on the negative. My university house mates were also constantly ranting about how shit the world was and moaning about fashionable people and pop music and how it's all a load of rubbish, while sitting there playing on the PlayStation and smoking weed until 4 in the morning. They would call people "sell outs" and I started to believe everything they were saying. It took a while for me to realise how toxic this was. I didn't want to ignore all the issues that were going on in the world, but I wanted to approach it in a different way. I reflected on the moment on the dancefloor when everyone turned, looked and laughed at me. What did I do? I laughed with them. I shifted my focus. I decided to focus on some of the hilarity of the things George Bush said at the time. I found an image of him on the phone, but the phone was upside down. I decided to paint it on a large canvas and everyone who walked past laughed. I sold that painting in an exhibition for £250 and subsequently sold 3 more for £1500. In hindsight, I shouldn't have made fun of him, because I know what it's like to be on the receiving end of it. I only did the one painting and decided that was enough. I had to move onto a different topic, so I explored the spiritual in abstract expressionism instead. I've changed a lot since then and I know that my frustration towards Bush was disempowering.

Art and other creative outlets are so powerful. Many songs, films and paintings have changed the world. They have created movements that open minds and start revolutions. Those artists have listened to their intuition and acted when they were guided to. They have changed the industry and used their creativity to create good in the world. You also have this power. You have the power to inspire.

ACTION POINTS

- Understand that you have your own power.
- Focus on the positives
- Don't take yourself too seriously

CHAPTER EIGHT
MORE DOORS OF SYNCHRONICITY – ACCEPT AND ADAPT

When I think back to the album that I recorded and the doors that opened for me, I never thought that it would take me on a journey to explore living with Erb's Palsy. I made a couple of music videos, and they were uploaded onto YouTube and other platforms. One day I received a message from a lady in America who said that her daughter also has Erb's Palsy. We got talking and she invited me over to play a gig at a venue where her daughter goes to learn music and perform with bands. It was called School of Rock (they have several of these across America). This was an amazing opportunity, and I was very grateful to be asked. I hopped on a plane and took a trip to Philadelphia, USA. My mum and dad came along for the ride too. I had never met anyone else with Erb's Palsy. I thought I was the only one. My parents had never spoken to other parents who had been through the same thing. It was very difficult for them, as it bought up feelings that hadn't risen for many, many years. As difficult as this was, it was definitely a healing process. I could write a whole book on my experience with Erb's Palsy, maybe I will one day. But the reason I'm telling you this is because Synchronicity was working right before my eyes.

I had taken action. I made an album. I filmed two music videos and had them uploaded online and it opened this exciting new door. At the time, my vision was to be a famous musician, but that's not where it led me. I wasn't to know this, but all of this was happening for a reason. All these actions were forming part of the bigger picture. After the School of Rock gig, I was invited to attend a UBPN Camp in St Louis, USA. UBPN stands for United Brachial Plexus Network. The camp happens every other year and it's designed to help and advise other people and families living with Erb's Palsy / Brachial Plexus Injury. I was flown out there for free to play some songs, speak about my injury and hopefully inspire a few people. Again, at the time I didn't know what this would lead to. I attended the camp in 2009 and loved every minute. I was still so focused on becoming rich and famous, I didn't really think too much about the Erb's Palsy. It was however incredible to talk to people who have struggled like me.

As time passed, I was performing less music and I was losing inspiration. I pretty much gave up on the idea of music, as I explained earlier. It wasn't until 2017 that I had a new idea. What if I set up a blog, Instagram, Website, Twitter feed and YouTube channel talking about my life with Erb's Palsy. I don't know what triggered it, but I was fired up and I decided to start working out. I have no idea why.

Working out in the gym had always been pretty awkward for me. I was embarrassed and didn't feel like I belonged there. The left side of my body is a lot weaker than my right, and I thought that I looked weird working out because I'm lop sided. I had a really bad view of myself. I thought I would start sharing exercises I did at the gym, in a way, to expose and to reveal to everyone WHY I look weird working out. Why I can lift 15kg with my right arm and only 2kg with my left. I started posting online and instantly people just like me started telling me about their stories. I looked fear in the face, and that's how I started a blog, YouTube and Instagram called Beating BPI (www.beatingbpi.com). I was terrified to expose myself like this, but people with Erb's Palsy really appreciated it. So I posted more content. People started sharing their stories with me and I decided to share them too. My feed became more about others than it did about me and it felt great. I don't know why I was doing this. It certainly wasn't to be famous. I just felt that I had to do it.

One day I started to think about how I could raise money for Erb's Palsy charities, as sadly not a lot of people fund them. I decided it would be a good idea to have a word or phrase that people could use on a T-Shirt. I had recently written an article for a magazine. They asked me to write something positive on a sheet of paper and hold it up for a photograph. I took the letters ERBS and wrote

E – Empowered

R – Resilient

B – Brave

S – Strong

Hundreds of people with Erb's Palsy started doing the same online and tagging me. It was mind blowing. Two people even had it tattooed on their arms. I wrote an article for my blog Beating BPI called 'Accept/Adapt,' which is about accepting who we are, accepting our injury and adapting to show the world what we can do if we put our mind to it. I thought these would be really good phrases to use on a range of clothing. I made some designs and found a 'print on demand' company to sell the apparel. I wanted 100% of the profits to go to the charity to help raise both money and awareness.

This sparked another idea. What if I make a documentary about Erb's Palsy? I studied a bit of film and photography at university. I know how to edit. This will be easy. I started reaching out to people with the injury and so many people wanted to get involved. I filmed a nerve surgeon, physiotherapist, professional boxer, professional NFL player, fashion designer and many more inspiring people. Because there was so much to talk about, I decided to release these as stand-alone episodes online. I was also asked back to UBPN Camp in 2019 and to join the Board of Directors. I said yes to this, but due to many other commitments I resigned after a year. If I do something, I want to do it properly. I had just become a father and I wanted to give all of my time to my family. It was my priority, so I took a step back so someone else could do the job properly. I was very grateful for the opportunity, but sorry I couldn't fulfil the role.

Why am I telling you this? Well, one day it struck me like a bolt of lightning. Everything made sense and I could see how everything in my life came together. I could see all the "chance meetings" coming together to get me to where I am today. When I took action to make an album, my vision was to be a rock star. What really happened was it opened a door for me to heal. It opened a door which I described earlier as being well and truly shut. I didn't like looking at myself in the mirror and seeing my arm. I didn't like looking at photos of my arm, as the first thing I looked at was how it hangs and how odd I look. Deep down, I was still holding onto the things the kids said to me at school. Subconsciously, I wanted to be rich and famous to hide what I was truly feeling. I didn't love myself. I wanted others to love me. I wanted them to give me their love and energy so that I could "love myself". Sadly, this kind of self-love is driven by ego and not acceptance. When we truly accept and love ourselves, we don't need acceptance from others.

My music was a success. It was successful because it opened doors for me to inspire others and to help them with their journey living with Erb's Palsy. I still very much enjoy making music and I still write, record and gig. However, I'm not doing it for the same reason I did in the beginning. I'm doing it because it brings me joy. If I'm completely honest with myself, I knew deep down music was not going to be the end goal. It served its purpose and I'm forever grateful. I do however hear you ask, "If I focused and acted more on music, would I have made it?" Yes, to a certain extent I probably would have. But I don't like to force things to be. It's very empowering when you follow and listen to your heart. Everything just fits. It's not a struggle. I have tried to force things in the past and I have learned to let things go when it becomes an internal fight. The following quote from The Celestine Prophecy summed it all up for me. "Once you learn what life is about, there is no way to erase the knowledge. If you try and do something else with your life, you will always sense that you are missing something." I got the feeling of missing something when I was trying to force things to happen in my life. As soon as I started to understand what my life was about.

I also play in an alternative rock band called Jacklines. It was the Law of Attraction and Synchronicity how this band came to be. I was getting a bit lonely gigging on my own. I visualised playing in a band and asked the Universe for some help. I didn't know at the time that one of my friends who I played cricket with also played guitar and sang. We decided to get together and jam. It was good fun and I enjoyed playing the songs we created. I put an advert in the local music shop for a bass player and a few days later I received a call. I invited him to come along for a jam to see if we worked well together. He was a lovely guy, and he joined the band straight away. The three of us could all play a range of instruments, so we mixed it up a bit. I would play guitar and sing and then we would rotate. After a while I decided I wanted to just stay on the guitar, so we advertised for a drummer. Again, a few days later I had a text message from a guy called Rudi and invited him along for a jam. He was from Slovakia and could barely speak a word of English. I thought he was cool, and to me, it didn't matter about the language thing. Music has its own language and as long as we connected musically, it didn't matter. One of the band members decided he wasn't a good fit, so he didn't join the band. It started to become a bit difficult. There were personality clashes and we ended up calling it a day.

A few months later I was on a stag-do weekend (weekend bachelor party) in Wales. I ended up meeting three wonderful friends on that stag-do. We just clicked and formed wonderful friendships. I was talking to a guy called James and he was telling me about the guitars that he owns. I couldn't believe it when he told me that he had a Taylor T5. I had the exact guitar at home. It's not a particularly common guitar. We decided to swap numbers and meet up to have a jam. The musical connection was instant. We just gelled together. We started writing a few songs and discussed getting a drummer. I put a few adverts out and left it to the Universe.

One day, I was having a coffee with my mum and I spotted Rudi in the corner of my eye. He didn't see me, but I took it as a sign to get in touch with him. It was over a year since we had met, and his English had developed dramatically. We met up, jammed and it just felt right. Nothing was forced. He said he worked with a guy who also plays guitar but would be happy to play the bass. We invited him along and his energy was incredible. He just took our songs to another level. Every time we meet and play music it just feels amazing. After a few years gigging and recording, Rudi said he was returning to Slovakia. We were sad, but we respected his decision and understood.

I was thinking about how we could continue the band without him. I thought back to our very first live performance as a band. We played an open mic night in a local town called Daventry. I was chatting to a guy called Karl, who is also a superb musician. I specifically remember him saying, "You guys sound freaking awesome. Jacklines will be huge. If you ever need a drummer, let me know." I hadn't spoken a word to him since, but I found his number on my phone and gave him a call. He's still our drummer today.

Jacklines formed through a string of synchronistic events. Events which happened because I acted on my intuition and gut feelings. I loved Rudi's energy when we first met. Despite not speaking the same language. The Universe lined up a year after our first meeting and we started an exciting journey together. I let the Universe deliver. What were the chances of meeting James on a drunken weekend in Wales? What were the chances of his having the same rare guitar as me? What were the chances of Rudi having a friend who was looking for a band, who happened to be an incredible bass player?

The thing I learned from this experience is that we must act on our intuition. We have had our music played on local BBC Introducing radio stations and played some cool gigs. We are certainly not famous. We do however LOVE playing music together and love the energy it creates. Why are we not a famous band who have sold millions of records? Well, that's an interesting question. I haven't cleared my limiting beliefs that I spoke about earlier. We are too old to breakthrough as a band now. I'm almost 40. Karl (the drummer) is too busy with other bands. I have 2 children. James has a daughter now. I'm not sure I could cope with life on the road. I would miss my family and I like my structure. Deep down, this is my belief. There is no way I could be successful while this is in my belief system. That's ok though. My dreams have changed and I'm at peace with that. I could spend time clearing my beliefs and re programme myself, but my vision and life is currently focused on something different. As I said earlier, I'm not a believer in forcing things to be. There's a difference between inspired action and forcing things. When the Universe is working with you, it feels right and becomes easy. When you step into the flow, you notice synchronicities which are signs that you are doing the right thing. You meet the right people, and you are in the right place at the right time. Maybe there is still room for music in my life. When I get the nudge, I'll act.

ACTION POINTS

- Don't try to force things to be
- Go where you are guided to go
- Be ok with dreams changing

CHAPTER NINE
UNDERSTANDING EMOTIONS

Some people are certainly more emotional than others. They are afraid of their emotions and can't stand the thought of facing them. We are very lucky to have a built-in guidance system, but many of us don't really know how to use it to our advantage. It can be really scary to let yourself feel vulnerable and open up, because when we do, sometimes it can be a bit unpredictable.

Some people call me a little emotional or over sensitive. Maybe you are a bit like me in that sense. As I grew up, many people would say that I need to develop thicker skin, or even worse I need to man up (which can have a negative impact on many aspects of a boy's life). I guess I can be a bit of a worrier. I like to try and organise things and I've become someone who likes to have a place for everything. This has certainly developed over time, and I guess it happened due to difficult things that have happened in the past and I'm trying to make sure it doesn't happen again. I'm always asking questions. I'm generally in tune with my emotions and I try my best to let them guide me. It's not always easy to do that, as sometimes we can't distinguish if it's our heart or head speaking. However, it's important to ride your emotions and let them play out, otherwise the pressure builds and our personalities and outlook on life can be slightly jaded, due to the fear of expressing our feelings. I've put together five reasons why I think we need to listen to our emotions, which will hopefully help you have a happier life. They will also help you notice more synchronicities and get you clear, to allow the Law of Attraction to work with you.

Emotions are your guidance system

It might sound simple, but your emotions let you know how you feel about situations. They are there to guide you. We know the feeling when we have done something bad. We also know what it feels like to make a good decision. Our emotions are there to help us make the right decision. We all want to feel happy, but we ride through so many different emotions each day. I don't think it's possible to stay completely happy 100% of the time. What we can do however, is notice how we feel and if we are becoming angry, stressed, or upset, we can shift our focus onto something happier. It's not healthy to ignore emotions and brush things under the carpet, but we are definitely in control of how we act on our emotions. When we do something good, it makes us feel good. When we do something bad, it makes us feel bad. We know we are onto a good thing because we feel it. Use your emotions to guide you and help make decisions. We can choose to respond, rather than react. Your emotions and the way that you FEEL, attract things to you.

Emotions will heal you

Processing how you feel will help you heal your life. Often, we bury how we feel, we don't confront our emotions and it all bottles up inside and eventually something will break. It's completely fine to feel how you feel. If you need to cry for no reason, then do it. You need to let it out. It will make you feel better. We tend to ignore things and pretend that everything is okay. Feel each emotion you have and try to understand why you feel them. Imagine your emotions as a line which starts at anger or depression and finishes with happiness and joy. To get to the ultimate feeling of happiness, you need to process all the other stuff before you can truly experience happiness. Try not to put pressure on other people to make you happy. You need to be at a point where you love yourself enough not to worry what others think. A big healing process is being at one with your emotions. Watch and listen to things that make you happy. Make an effort to stay positive.

You know how you truly feel

Listen to your feelings and make decisions based on them. We have all experienced situations where you say things such as, "I had a feeling I shouldn't have done that." It's important to listen to those feelings and take action based on them. The difficulty is knowing if it's your head talking or your emotions. Practising mindfulness will certainly clear your head and help you make better decisions. If you feel that something isn't right, then it isn't. You owe it to yourself to be happy and to listen. If you are in a relationship that you don't want to be in, you have a feeling that it's not right and often ignore it. If you make decisions based on your feelings, then it will ultimately lead you to a happier life.

Live from the heart

If you live from the heart, you will be ultimately end up in a happier place. You will make better decisions and attract happier people. If you keep all your negative emotions bottled up, they will always be there, until one day it all just comes pouring out in an unpredictable way. We all deserve to be happy, even if you've been through rough times. Know that this is just your current situation and that you have the power to change.

You will find clarity

For some of us, finding clarity can take a lifetime. Sometimes we think we have found it and then another rough life experience gets thrown into the mix and the clear blue skies become cloudy again. We are all happier when the skies are blue, and the sun is out. We need to do what we can to stay in that place. Listening to your emotions will help you stay in clarity because as you process the emotions you are letting go of negativity, rather than keeping it locked up like a caged animal.

It's not an easy journey and there is no "one size fits all" method to it. When you feel anger rush through your body it becomes an overwhelming feeling which can result in bad decision making. Imagine your emotions as a mountain and at the top of the mountain is your joy. Getting there will be difficult. It will be full of tough challenges mixed with beautiful moments and beautiful views. There will be times when you will want to give up and go back. There will be times which are unpredictable and moments when you think time stands still. Then one day you realise that you have reached the top. You look back at your journey and see everything that you have accomplished and can be proud of your achievements.

I like to use the power of my M.I.N.D, which stands for My Intuitive Navigational Device. The power of our mind is unlimited, and we have more power than we know. When we listen to our Intuitive Navigational Device we arrive at our destination with ease. It works a bit like a Sat-Nav. When we type in our destination, the GPS works out the best route and if an obstruction occurs, it gives you another clear route. Your M.I.N.D works in exactly the same way. When you DECIDE what you want, you ask the Universe to help you. Often, we don't act on the signs and nudges. Imagine getting in your car, programming the Sat-Nav to the destination you want to go to and then just sitting there on the drive. Alternatively, you start your car, go down the road and ignore everything the Sat-Nav says. You may get to where you want to go, but it will take you longer. Learning to use your M.I.N.D properly will give you the shortest route to your goals.

The issue is that we don't trust the Sat Nav. We don't trust our nudges from the Universe or our intuition. We don't believe that the Universe will give us what we want. Learning to let go and trust is a huge part of acting on your intuition. Once you have mastered this, you will start manifesting more into your life.

ACTION POINTS

- Let yourself be emotional
- Use your emotions as a guidance system
- Enjoy the journey
- Use your M.I.N.D to reach your goals

CHAPTER TEN
SELF-MOTIVATION

Every day in the classroom I hear kids say, "Sir, I can't do this". Sometimes the kids say it before they've even tried! I remember one day I'd heard it one too many times. I stopped the class and asked the pupils to gather round and I said the following, "I'm hearing too many of you saying you can't do this. Some of you haven't even tried yet. I'm going to tell you something that I've never told any other pupil. I was born with a paralysed left arm. The doctors told me I'd never move it, never play an instrument, never play sport above a basic level and never be able to do any DIY around the house. I refused to believe this. They told me I can't. I told myself I can. I play drums and guitar in a band, I have released music and gigged around the country and even overseas. I played county cricket for Northamptonshire until I was 18 and I'm standing here teaching you Design Technology and an expert in DIY. I will not accept you telling me that you CAN'T do this task" They looked at me in disbelief and got on with the task. Not one of them said, "I can't do it" again. They all completed the task to a high standard.

But how do people get motivated? Do people have an epiphany? Do motivated people come from positive backgrounds? Do they come from poor backgrounds? Does motivation come from being educated? Does it come from parents and their beliefs? And does that then influence your beliefs? It's not often that people just wake up one morning and decide to change their life. There's a little voice inside of us that really wants to do something and then there's another voice that stops you or makes excuses.

I dislike the expressions, "a leopard can never change its spots" and "you can't teach an old dog new tricks." These give us limited belief and stop us before we've even tried to do anything. We are so lucky to be born in the age of opportunity. We have free education and a free health service. Legally, you must be in education until you are 18. Think about that for a moment... You MUST be educated. You MUST be given the tools to be successful. Yet, I hear people say, "I hate school, school is boring. I can't wait to leave. What's the point of this?" You may not enjoy school, or you may not have enjoyed it when you were younger, but there are people in the world who would do anything to be given those opportunities.

No matter how many people stand in front of you to try to inspire you, it must come from you. Your motivation and your happiness are your responsibility. I can stand here all day long and tell you to get motivated, but that just sounds like I'm nagging you and then you're likely to resist. You can blame others if you want, but where is that going to get you? Time pointing the finger and sulking is wasted time, it's wasted energy that you can be using to make your life better.

You have a choice. Everything you do comes down to a choice. What you had for breakfast, what clothes you put on this morning. You can choose to be a positive and enthusiastic person. Some people aren't enthusiastic because they don't know what to do in life, they think "I'm not good at anything, I don't know what to do, I'm bored". A friend of mine was quite brutal and said, "only boring people get bored". Be inquisitive, go and try things out, you may develop a new passion or a hidden talent. What would you do if you knew you couldn't fail? Be brave and give it a go. Listen to what your gut is telling you and act on it.

What holds us back? What stops us from starting? I found that confidence and discipline are two of the main factors. These two things are very hard things to master. Confidence is like any other skill. The hardest thing is taking the first step. It's like doing a parachute jump. Taking the step out of a plane that is flying through the air seems crazy! It's only because we've never done it before. As soon as the parachute opens, it's bliss and you want to do it again. The more you do it, the more confident you become. Like any skill, with practice you become better and then over time, you become a master of it.

Discipline can be tough. We always make excuses. Not enough time, not enough money, I won't be able to do that. Or we start something new, do a week of it and then stop. Why do we do that?

Too hard? It'll take too long? Too much effort... I hate it when I hear my pupils say, "Ugghh, but that's effort sir" Laziness is the foundation of mediocrity.

I found that you need to find time to be still, to listen. Make a decision and make it happen. It frustrates me when people say, "I always wanted to play the piano." Ok... then play it. Order a keyboard online, go onto YouTube and find some lessons. Make a start. What's stopping you? It sounds brutal but, get on with it! If you live a life saying, "I always wanted to do that" you'll never do anything and you may live a life of regret. When you do finally make the decision to do the thing you want to do, who knows what doors will open, what friends you will make and new opportunities you never imagined. Life is incredible and it's meant to be a journey of excitement, joy and full of wonderful experiences.

When I went to school, I developed a real passion for cricket. My father played cricket and from a baby I would go up to the local cricket ground every Saturday and as a family, we would watch him play. When I was at school my passion really started to grow and I started to become a really good cricketer. I wanted to play for the school team called the 'Colts'. We had a Colts 1 XI, 2 XI and 3 XI. I kept trying to improve my game. Even when my friends and I were playing cricket in the playground at lunch time I would really try hard. One day the coach told me he was going to give me trials for the team. I was really excited and somewhat nervous. When the day finally arrived, I went to the trials and to my joy I actually made it into the team. I only played for the 3 XI, but I was still in the team.

The next step for me was making it into the Colts 1 XI which was better than the Colts 2 XI. The following year I started playing and I worked my way up from the 3 XI to the 2 XI and then eventually the 1 XI. I remember that I was on the front page of the local newspaper because I had pretty much single-handedly won a match for us against a team that we had not beaten for 30 years. I got 6 wickets for 12 runs off 8 overs (That won't make sense to anyone who doesn't follow cricket, but it's awesome). I was pretty pleased with myself to say the least. After this victorious moment the coach put me through for county trials. I failed to get in, but I kept on working at it until I made the squad. I ended up playing for my county from under 13's to under 18's. I then went on to captain my university cricket team, albeit for one match, but at least I can say I captained the team. I was Vice Captain for a year, and I captained my local village 1 XI team for several years. The reason that I am writing about this story is because it shows you what determination can do. It proves that the limiting belief that the doctors had in their head, can't change the image that I had in my head. If you want to go and do something, then do it.

A similar experience happened with swimming. I couldn't swim very well as a child because my arm was not strong enough and I didn't have the range of movement. I used to swim round in circles because I would do it one handed. My parents decided to pay for swimming lessons for me. I was afraid of water, and to be honest I still don't like deep water. It never stopped me though. I was determined to do it. My mother told me that if I could do a whole length of the pool, she would buy me a skateboard. All my friends had a skateboard and I wanted one too. I think my mother had doubts about me doing a whole length because she didn't really want me to have a skateboard and at the time, I could barely swim a width, let alone a length. I started to swim. It must have looked like miles and miles of water to me, but I did it. I managed to get from one end of the pool to the other, and my mother had to take me to the shop and buy me my first skateboard. I wanted the board so much I made sure I did that length no matter how hard it was.

When I was at school, we had swimming races. We were all in our 'houses.' I was in a house called Mountbatten, named after Earl Mountbatten. One of the others was Churchill, obviously after Winston. I can't remember the other names of the houses, but there were four. It was in the moment that I'm about to describe which really knocked the confidence out of me. It was a moment when I wondered why I had this problem with my arm. Why wasn't I like everyone else? Thankfully, I now know why, and I'm glad I'm not like everyone else. We were having relay swimming races. I was new to the school and had never done anything like this before. To be honest I didn't know what the hell was going on, no one told me what I had to do. I think everyone just assumed that I knew. We all lined up; I was third in the line. The gun fired and the first guys dived into the pool and swam as fast as they could. I couldn't believe how fast they were swimming. There was no way I could swim that fast. It got to my turn, and I just jumped in the pool. I didn't know how to dive like the other guys. I put so much effort into swimming; I was going as fast as I could, you have no idea how hard I was trying. People were yelling at me, 'Go on!

Swim!' I WAS swimming. I was swimming as fast as I physically could. By the time that I swam my two lengths, the other teams had finished the race, and there was still the fourth person in my team to go. I was so embarrassed. From that moment on I wondered why I had this problem in my arm. I dreaded that race every year. I felt like I had let everyone down, and of course, they were all angry at me because I lost the race for them. I started to dislike school from then and people started calling me names. I felt different from all the others. Why wasn't I fitting in? Why wasn't I one of the 'cool kids? I started to look at myself in the mirror and look at the physical difference of my arm and started to hate it. It was standing out like it never had before. There were times that I just didn't want to go into school. The more I didn't want to go, the worse it got at school. This was my first experience of the Law of Attraction, but at the time I didn't realise.

My time on this planet is unique, as is yours. I now choose to believe that my injury was a gift. Sometimes we need to actually stand back and look at ourselves, look at what we have and decide which path we are going to walk down. I'm choosing to walk down the positive road where I hope to inspire and educate people in the same position as me, rather than the negative path where I choose to feel victimised. Yes, I agree it can be difficult. But what can you do today to feel better about the situation you are in?

ACTION POINTS

- Take action – Just do it!
- Work at becoming clear of limiting beliefs and negativity

- Become self-motivated by using role models, positive music or inspiring videos
- Do anything to make you take that first step

CHAPTER ELEVEN
DO YOU TRUST YOUR PARKING SENSORS?

I was reversing into a car parking space at work last week and my parking sensors went off. It happens every day, but I usually turn them off and park without them as the car automatically turns down whatever I'm listening to on the radio. For some reason, this time I didn't turn it off. As the beeping got faster, I decided to stop, even though I knew I had lots of room still behind me. For some reason I didn't trust them. I didn't want to go further back, just in case there was something else there. I used them once before and it didn't sense that something was there and I ended up gently reversing into an object.

I thought about how we are a bit like this with our goals. If we think of the car parking space as the final target, we are trying to manoeuvre ourselves into a specific space. Sometimes we don't see better or even easier spaces to move into. Think of your goals like this. Be open to the possibility that you can achieve even better things than you imagined. There may be better things for you. We have warning signs, or nudges from the Universe, but we ignore them. Sometimes we get into the space, but we still have further to go and for some reason we stop, even though we know we can go that little bit further. It reminds me of another Joe Vitale quote when he says, "dare something worthy". We are guilty of setting limitations on our expectations. We don't think that we are good enough, so we set the bar just high enough that we can jump over it, but don't always go that extra mile. We set off aiming to achieve a goal and then give up or go a certain distance and then decide it's enough. We must learn to trust our parking sensors. Listen to the Universe and trust that the Law of Attraction, along with your inspired action, will get you to where you want to go.

One of the first positive experiences of the Law of Attraction I remember was when I was doing my GCSE exams at only sixteen years old. I wrote down on a piece of paper exactly the grades I wanted to get. I asked the Universe to help me and put the paper under a crystal. I wrote the following…

Art - A*
Physical Education – A
Maths - B
Design Technology – C
English - C
English Literature – C
Science - C
Religious Studies - D

The reason I didn't write down A* for all of my subjects was because I was doing what we call 'intermediate' or 'foundation' level in English, Science, and Design Technology, due to my dyslexia. The highest grade I could get was a C. I did a slightly higher level in Maths and the highest grade I could get was a B. I could get an A* for Physical Education but I said to myself that I would be more than happy with an A. I also said that I would be happy with a D for Religious Studies because at the time I wasn't too interested in it, and if I was to get all these good grades then it didn't matter so much about the D grade. I'll be honest, I did no revision for Religious Studies, so a D was a miracle.

I sat the exams a few months later, let go and waited. On results day, I phoned the school and the teacher read out my grades one at a time. To my delight, they were exactly the same as I'd written down a month earlier. I was shocked, I couldn't believe it. It was a miracle. I started to believe that there was something in this "ask the Universe" thing. What I realise now is that I set an intent and let go.

You may look at my exam grades and think, "Hold on, he got a C for GCSE Design Technology and now he's going to be Head of Department." Or "He only got C in English and he's writing a book!" I wonder that too sometimes. I'm also dyslexic. Does that mean I can't do these things? Not being a straight A student and still making it to Head of Department and writing a book, is, in my opinion, is absolute success. I've removed any limiting beliefs that I would never be able to do those things and worked hard at it. I wasn't the best student in the world. Not that that I was naughty or anything. I just wanted to do what interested me and get better at the things I was good at. My academia wasn't as good as my creativity. I wanted to make things, paint, act, play cricket, play my drums. I wanted the fun stuff… and still do.

However, as I got older, I wanted to learn more, and because I wanted to learn more, I found it easier. I have learned so much in the past 15 years. Probably more than I did when I was at school or university. We are so fortunate that we can teach ourselves new skills. We can use YouTube, sign up to courses, do online courses, buy "how to" DVDs and so much more. I taught myself how to play guitar and now I have 2 albums and 2 EP's, and I have played hundreds of gigs. I was even told I physically wouldn't be able to do that! There isn't really an excuse. If you want to do something. Do it. It's as simple as that. The thing that gets in our way is our confidence. Somewhere along the line we get the confidence knocked out of us. Whether that's due to bullies at school, rubbish teachers, parents, or whoever. Sadly, this can stop us fulfilling our dreams. We have subconscious and often conscious beliefs that we can't do something before we even give it a go! We say things like "I'd never be able to do that, there's no point." Can you see what you are doing here? Why not give it a go? What's the worst that can happen? Are you worried someone will laugh at you? So what if they do? You are not doing it for them, you are doing it for you. Do yourself a favour today. Do something you have always wanted to do. Even if you can't do it today for some reason. Take some action and make it happen tomorrow. You don't have to be an expert. It's all about the joy of doing it and learning new skills. Who knows where this new road will take you. Learning is a key that opens many doors. The more you learn, the more doors will open for you. You are never too old to learn. This is why I really dislike the saying, "you can't teach old dog's new tricks." Talk about limiting beliefs!

We find all sorts of excuses not to chase our dreams. Two weeks ago, I had an idea come to me to write a book. So, I'm doing it. I'm a full-time teacher, Head of Year, I have a toddler, I have just done an online parents evening which lasted 3 hours straight after a long day. Rather than playing on the PlayStation or watch TV for an hour before going to bed, I decided to write. Little bits every day add up. If I write a page a day, by the end of the year I would have a 365-page book. When we are inspired, we WANT to do it. You make time. It's a joyful process and it feels exciting. I'm so fired up about writing this book and sharing my stories. I look forward to having an hour or two in the evening when I can just sit and write. It's not arduous in any way. It's fun. Life SHOULD be fun. Unfortunately, sometimes, if we are not aware, other people's negativity can influence us. It's important that we monitor what is in our lives and make adjustments if necessary. Making a start can be the hardest thing, as we get stuck in routines. Starting today, make a new routine for yourself. YOU are in charge.

ACTION POINTS

- Trust your parking sensors
- Notice the signs, no matter how small
- Allow the good in / Notice the good
- Listen to your gut feelings. Follow them without doubt

one text here. Insert chapter one text here. Insert chapter one text here.

CHAPTER TWELVE
YOU ARE A VERY RICH YOUNG MAN

I never let my Erb's Palsy stop me. Don't get me wrong, there have been times when I've really struggled emotionally, physically and mentally. But I was given it for a reason. There's no point in being angry. I don't call it a disability, because even if I can't do things the way other people do, I find a way around it. My injury was all part of the synchronicities playing out in my life. Let me explain…

I was born with Brachial Plexus Injury / Erb's Palsy. My parents were devastated and didn't understand why this was happening. Why should they? Someone did this to their baby. They were angry and confused, so they decided to take legal action. This was in the 1980's, so there was no internet or support groups around. The idea was that the money from the court case could help pay for things such as operations and technology I may need to help me with day-to-day tasks. It also funded my education. One of the schools I went to, I met my lifelong friend Trystan who helped me with my music. I ended up going back to that school to train as a teacher and I also met my wife there. None of this would have happened if I wasn't born with Erb's Palsy. How can I be mad about having this injury when it has given me so much? Was it all one big coincidence? What I did without realising was take inspired action. Because I did that, I opened even more opportunities for synchronicities to occur, which led me to a place of happiness, with my dreams easily unfolding before me.

I mentioned a moment ago that my parents took legal action. I do understand why they did this, but it's a difficult thing for me to wrap my head around because I had no say in it. One of my earliest memories was being in a strange room full of people. It was like no other room I had been in before. There was a man in a funny wig at the front, who was looking at us. I remember a few ladies all staring at me, and one was wearing leopard skin print trousers. During the previous few days, I had been in and out of other boring rooms talking to men in suits. I had no idea what was going on, but I could sense nervous energy around me and something important was happening. It was also really, really boring. When we were sat in front of funny wig man, he suddenly said, "Matthew, please can you come to the front". My mum frantically grabbed my hand and we sat in a chair near him. He started asking me questions about cricket. I had NO idea what was happening. I tried to answer the questions as well as an 8-year-old could. He then said, "Well Matthew, you are now a very rich young man."

We had won the case and I was awarded £150000 compensation. This was one of the first cases ever won to do with Erb's Palsy. I clearly remember someone saying, "no, we don't want this in the newspapers." My parents had spent a lot of money on this case and the judge told them to take £10000 and the rest will be handed over to me when I was 18 years old. The money was held in a trust fund and if I needed any of it, I would have to write to the people looking after it to release what I needed.

Would I have taken legal action? I spoke earlier about how this was Synchronicity in action. If it wasn't for my Erb's Palsy, I wouldn't be where I am today. The money paid for my education and through that, I trained as a teacher and met my best friend and wife. I often think about the doctors and the midwives who delivered me. They would NEVER want to injure a baby on purpose. A mistake was made. What happened to them after this incident? I have no idea. As much as my parents were traumatised, I know they will have been affected too. Did they carry this around with them all their life? My guess is that they did. For which I can only say sorry. But I also want to say thank you. Thank you for saving my life and thank you for this opportunity to inspire and for being a part in my life's coincidences.

Growing up my parents often argued about money. Even now, my parents are convinced they can't afford things. Even though they have just bought two new cars and have no mortgage. When I was 18, I tried to invest my money in property. I renovated a few houses and sold them for a profit. I wanted to be a property mogul, but I was just a kid. I wanted the money to pile up. I wanted to buy more, sell more, make more and have more. I made a few bad investments over the years and sadly I lost most of it. The only thing I had left was one property which I was renting out. I had no money in the bank, but there was around £60000 equity in this house. Which was only because I rented it out for several years and property value increased dramatically.

How did I end up losing the money? Subconsciously I believed that I didn't have enough money. I grew up around the energy of "not enough". We struggled a lot. We nearly lost the family house and we had cars repossessed. While all of this was happening, I had £140000 sat waiting for me. It was all sinking in. The worry of losing it all, caused me to lose it all. I created this situation with my subconscious beliefs. It took me a long time to wipe this belief and occasionally I still slip back into this mindset. When I catch myself doing this, I quickly clear it and redirect my thoughts. When my wife and I decided to buy our family home, I cashed in on the property I rented out and put it all down as a deposit. We have a beautiful home, and we are truly grateful. In the five years we have been here, the house price has gone up £85000.

I earn a decent wage; my wife and I have some savings and we have no debt (apart from our reasonably small mortgage). Financially, I'm doing just fine. Can I have more money? Of course. We can always have more money. Do I want more money? Sure. But as I mentioned earlier in this book, I am no longer chasing money. It's not my main focus anymore. I don't seem to attract money as easily as other things in my life and here's why.

- I still have limiting beliefs
- I haven't properly cleared my past
- I still fear losing it
- I feel that I don't deserve it
- I worry that people will judge me if I was rich

Maybe some of these points resonate with you. If they do, then you will also need to clear your beliefs about money. These kinds of beliefs hold us back from attracting in more. Money is just a vibration like everything else, but we fear it.

Growing up, my mother would say, "don't tell ANYONE about your money. People will try and con you to take it from you and you'll end up losing everything we fought for. We fought hard for that money; you need to look after it". Reflecting on this now, I can totally see why I lost it all and why I have a fear of losing money, even now. I know that my mother was trying to protect me, and I completely understand why she was saying this to me, but these words are coming from a place of fear. Fear of losing everything, and that fear of losing everything came from the fact we almost DID lose everything in the past. We were trying to learn from the mistakes and not let it happen again, and that's a good thing. We should learn from our mistakes, but we also need to forgive the past and clear our limiting belief that this is the only way that it has to be.

We need to learn and then make changes. We shouldn't learn and then fall into the same pattern. Life is meant to be fun. Having money is fun! Many of us struggle with our relationship with money and sometimes our relationships can struggle because of money. So many arguments happen because of money. It can save lives and ruin lives. When we look deeper, it's a reflection of our belief. So, if you are in a situation right now where you don't have enough. What are your actual beliefs about money?

ACTION POINTS

- Work out what your limiting beliefs are about money. Once you identify these beliefs, reset them. Choose to believe something different
- Write down what you would buy if you could buy anything right now. How do you feel? Know that you deserve all of the things you desire… and more.

CHAPTER THIRTEEN
FOLLOWING CREATIVITY

The definition of the word 'create' is; "to bring into existence." When you say that you are not creative, you are not thinking of the bigger picture. You can CREATE the world around you, and you can make it as beautiful as you like. We often think of creativity in regards to an art form, but creativity is making something from nothing. You have the power to create the most incredible story ever written and that story is your life and your experiences. Our lives are one continuous moving picture, which changes depending on or expectations and intent. To me, that sounds like the most incredible piece of art that I have ever heard of. To be able to look at a work of art and watch it change depending on what we think. That is exactly what is happening with your life. The only question you need to ask is; What do I want to be in my picture?

18 months ago, I had an urge that I hadn't had for 19 years. I wanted to draw. I have a degree in Fine Art, but after I graduated, I lost all inspiration for the art world. I didn't see myself as an artist and I certainly would never have a career in it. I was on holiday with my wife, son, mother-in-law, and father-in-law. It was the first adventure we had after the first Covid lockdown in 2020. We were in a wooden hut in Devon, and I sat on the porch and drew the landscape as the sun was setting. It wasn't a very good drawing, but I wanted to continue. Something was telling me that I HAD to keep drawing. I always loved drawing portraits when I was studying art at school, so I decided to do a freehand drawing of my wife. I was really happy with the result, so I thought I would do a few more. I drew Dave Grohl, Peter Gabriel, and a few other of my idols. I posted them on Facebook and received many positive comments from friends and family.

It was drawing the portrait of Peter Gabriel that something clicked in me. I was completely absorbed in the process, and I wanted to make it look the best it could. I took my time and treated it like a mindfulness exercise. This portrait was a game changer for me. I started to receive messages from friends who wanted to have portraits done of their loved ones and even their pets. I couldn't believe it. Where did this come from? I had gone from drawing nothing in almost 19 years to taking portrait commissions pretty much overnight

The Universe was speaking to me, and I was listening. It's too easy to ignore these gut instincts. We find reasons not to. If I'm honest, I was nervous about drawing again. What if I was rubbish? What if people didn't like it? All these things and more went around my head, but I did it anyway. I am really proud of my artwork, and now I draw most evenings for an hour before I go to bed. It's time away from the screen and it's time for me to be mindful. When we think of meditation and mindfulness, we often believe that we have to sit quietly, cross legged with incense sticks burning. As nice as this is, mindfulness can be done anywhere. I get a similar feeling when I sit and play my guitar for an hour. It's my time and it's healing.

Since I started drawing again, I have completed over 40 portraits and made a bit of money. Money was never the intention, but it started flowing to me straight away. I decided to set up an Etsy shop to sell prints of my work. (You can see these at www.mattparsons.co.uk). An hour after I opened the shop, I got an order. Again, it's important to act when you have divine inspiration. I started making money without even trying. I had earned more money taking drawing commissions in a few weeks, than I had in years making music. The money started flowing to me because I wasn't making it the target. A strange thing happened when I started focusing on making more money from it. The money slowed down and basically stopped. Again, my limiting belief of money was kicking in. It's so important to eliminate all limitation from your subconscious, as it has a powerful effect of what you can manifest.

Creativity connects you to spirit and it can take many forms. You don't have to be an artist, musician, or author to be creative. I often hear people say, "I haven't got a creative bone in my body." If you have ever said that, you are keeping doors well and truly closed. You can always learn new skills and do it for the joy of doing it. Start an art class, start singing or dance lessons. What have you got to lose? When I started drawing again, I had no idea where it would take me, but it has already started opening doors…

ACTION POINTS

- If you have ever had an urge to learn a new skill, do it today
- What do you want in your picture? Make a list and do small things each day to make it happen

CHAPTER FOURTEEN
USE OF LANGUAGE

I recently did an online course about the use of language at school. It got me thinking about the language we use every day and how we inadvertently stop ourselves from bringing in what we want. Some of the following phrases are good and some bad. I want you to read them and consider how many of these you say and how often you say them. Also, think about how they resonate inside you. Are they positive? Are they negative? As you read them, you may find that there are others which are not on the list which spring to mind. Again, think about how the words sound and how they feel when we say them. Do you notice anything in your mind and body? Write next to them exactly how they make you feel.

"If you don't ask, you don't get"

"I want, never gets"

"Speak when you're spoken to"

"Admit it, you want something you can't have."

"You can't please everyone"

"Things happen for a reason"

"You get out what you put in"

"Do as I say, not as I do"

"You can't win them all"

"Expect the worst and you won't be let-down"

"Good things come to those who wait"

"Money doesn't grow on trees"

"I'm not made of money?"

"There's not enough to go around"

"That never happens to people like us"

"What goes around comes around"

"Yeah, good luck with that…"

"When hell freezes over"

"I can't believe it"

"I'm so old"

"Man up"

"I always wanted to do that"

"Time speeds up when you get older"

"You'll get what's coming to you"

"Make the most of it while it lasts"

When I was writing those phrases, I started thinking about how we respond to the everyday questions that come up in general conversation. Here are some of the replies that I've been guilty of saying. I wonder if you are guilty of saying them too.

"Yeah, I'm ok"

"Getting by"

"Plodding along"

"I'm too tired to do that"

"I haven't got the time to do that"

"I'm in such a rush"

"I can't be bothered"

"I'm so busy right now"

"Oh, joy" (sarcastically)

"You can't teach old dog's new tricks"

"All good things come to an end"

I make a conscious effort these days to respond in a positive way. If someone asks me how I am, I now reply by saying, "I'm great!". If I reply by moaning about the weather or how busy I am, then I am adding negativity to my life. It's not always easy though. Once we start on the negativity spiral, it soon goes out of control. I have experienced this in the workplace. Once one person starts moaning, sooner or later everyone else is. If I put out good vibes, it will come back to me. I'm not saying that I ignore my emotions. I just choose when to offload.

It's not healthy to hold everything in. Talking to someone is such an important healing process. If I rant to my work colleagues about my job, I'm fueling the fire of negativity. How do YOU talk to the people at work?

In the previous section I talked about how I started drawing again and selling prints of my work. When I get deliveries at home, I often keep the cardboard so that I can reuse it for packaging for when I sell my artwork. A few weeks ago, we had a huge delivery of flat pack furniture for the nursery for our new baby. We had loads of cardboard. As I was tidying up, I said to myself, "I'll keep this cardboard in case I sell some prints." Can you see what I did there? I caught myself saying, "in case I sell". I should have said, "I'll keep this cardboard for WHEN I sell some more prints." Small changes like this can have a massive impact on your life. The language we use has a huge effect on our beliefs. The more we say it, the more we believe it. The more we believe it, the more it's going to happen.

A few years ago, I was very stressed at work and I was making a conscious effort to meditate more. Mediation is so important, but for some reason, there is a bit of a stigma attached to it. For those people who practice mindfulness, they understand its importance and power. For those who have never tried it, or tried it once and said it didn't work, they are quick to dismiss it. I teach the dot.be Mindfulness in Schools course to the children at school. Some of the pupils really engage in it, while others (more often the boys) don't take it seriously and joke around. I've even experienced this in the staff room before. I have had fellow colleagues tease me about meditating and tell me that it's "girly".

One day, I decided to buy a mindfulness magazine called 'Planet Mindful.' It was a really interesting read, but as I was reading it, I felt that most of the articles were directed towards women. I looked in the back few pages and noticed that there was only one or two men who had written articles. I wrote to the editor and explained how I felt about this, and I attached an article that I had written called, "Real men practise mindfulness", which was about the negative experiences that I've had, when other men find out that I meditate. The editor loved my article, and it was published in the May 2019 edition. I was happy that it was published and hopefully it helped some of the men out there who are struggling with the "man-up" society.

A practical thing for you to do is to re-frame the way that you look at the world and the way that you communicate with others. For example, we can be guilty of moaning on a Sunday night about having to get up early to go to work. We say that we "hate Mondays'." Instead of thinking and focusing about how bad Monday mornings are. Think about the amazing weekend that you have had. Say, "thank you for another Monday and an opportunity to make some more money." In the middle of the week I often hear, "It's only Wednesday!" You could say, "only two days until the weekend!" However, the problem with this kind of talk, no matter how you re-frame it, is that you are not in the moment. You are focusing on the fact it's not the weekend and you count down the days, whilst not appreciating the moment you are in. By doing this, you miss synchronicities, and you are not being grateful for the present.

Re-framing can be a simple way to change your life. When we change our habits, we can start attracting more to us. Even the simplest of things such as, "I hate the rain," can be enough to bring in more things that you hate. Without rain, the planet as we know it, would not survive. Maybe there is something in the phrase, "if you can't say anything nice, don't say anything at all." It's all too easy to pass judgement and criticise but think about what you are putting out to the Universe. It feels great when you interact with someone who is positive. If you talk to someone and they leave with a smile on their face, then you have done something amazing today.

ACTION POINTS

- Be aware of the language that you use
- Re-frame the way that you see the world
- Use only positive words and phrases, as this will raise your energy and help you attract more joy into your life

CHAPTER FIFTEEN
DR JOE VITALE – INSPIRED ACTION

Sometimes you find a book that changes your life. You find an author who opens your eyes and mind and makes you see the world in a different way. I was introduced to the book and film The Secret by Rhonda Byrne in my early 20's. I was obsessed with it. I listened to the audiobook daily and watched the movie constantly. It really helped me understand the principles of the Law of Attraction. I was aware of the Law of Attraction, as my mother was always listening to Jerry and Esther Hicks audio recordings. When I watched The Secret, I was very much drawn to Joe Vitale's energy and his outlook on life. I ordered some of his books and loved each one. I was reading his blog one day and he was asking for submissions for stories about personal experiences with the Law of Attraction. I wrote something right away and submitted it. Over time I forgot all about it, until one day I was reading his book called 'Expect Miracles.' I was almost at the end of the book, and I was reading a story that sounded all too familiar. I suddenly realised that I was reading my own story! Joe had included my submission in his book! I had no idea that he published it. I was so excited. At the time I was going through a pretty dark period in my life, and this changed everything in an instant. Here's the extract from his book...

Matt's story is a great example of letting go and allowing good things to flow through your life.

I have experienced Law of Attraction in numerous areas of my life so far. Some of the time, I didn't even realise it was at work until I looked back and thought about the situations, I was in. Unfortunately, some of them were what we call 'negative' experiences, although now I think that they were all positive and useful for the feedback they provided.

I was born with a condition called Erb's Palsy, which meant my nerves were torn from my spine and my left arm was left paralysed. As I grew, doctors told my parents and me that I wouldn't be able to play any sport, swim or play any musical instruments. This was the image that they had in their head and what they had seen in others. However, the image I had for my life differed from my parents'.

I began swimming lessons, though I found it hard at first. I used to swim in circles because my right arm was a lot stronger than my left. I set my mind to swimming a whole length of the pool and one day I finally managed to do it. I also developed a passion for cricket at a young age. I wanted to play cricket for my county. I also wanted to be captain of my local village team. I focused and visualised with all my might. Eventually, my coach put me for county trials and I made it into the squad. I played semi-professional cricket for five years. I captained my university team and now, my local village team. I know that anything is possible if you put your mind to it. It only needs passion and emotion.

In the past, I've had negative experiences with bullying at school. At the time, I was focusing on the name calling and nasty actions that the other children would engage in. I now realise that my focus was attracting more of what I didn't want. It wasn't until one day that I just ignored them that it started to disappear and I became one of the popular kids at school. I also attracted exam results. I remember a month before my exams, I wrote down the grades that I wanted to receive. I asked the Universe and let it go. The results day arrived and to my amazement, my grades were exactly the same as the ones I had written down, prior to the tests.

I studied fine art at university and my focus was on the frustration with the world. I was painting subjects of war and terrorism. I wanted to make people aware that we need to make changes in the world. The problem was that it was dragging me down emotionally. My grades started to slip and I became very angry. I lived in a house with eight other people. I was suffering from sleepless nights. Two of my housemates were listening to very negative music and played it late at night and very loud. I was so depressed and I didn't know why. One day, I was looking at images of George Bush on the internet. I decided to paint this image in a cartoon fashion surrounded by fluffy clouds. My tutors hated it, but everyone else loved it. This was a turning point for me, as I realised that it was my perception and how I viewed things in my life that created my attitude and attracted my results.

I was approaching my subjects in a more comical way and my whole life changed. You see, when you focus on things with a passion it can affect your whole life. I had a call one day from a gallery; they wanted to show my art in an exhibition. I was attracting them because I had changed my thoughts and actions. I sold a painting before the exhibition had even opened and then went on to sell three more in the same month! I then attracted one of my dream cars a few months later and a holiday to New York for me, my girlfriends and my parents.

I'd been told all my life that I would never play any musical instruments. But one day, I felt inspired to pick up the guitar. I naturally picked it up the wrong way round. I was playing left-handed. I can't turn my arm over to play chords, but I can finger pick and strum. My parents bought me a left-handed guitar for one of my birthdays. While at University, I started to develop my song writing skills and recorded a demo album with a friend of mine who had a small recording studio. I started to really enjoy music and for the last two years, I've been writing and recording an album that I've poured my heart and soul into. My roommate works as a professional musician and his boss is a phenomenal musician and has worked with some amazing people. One day, I asked the Universe for him to work with me on my new album. I came home one night and I spoke to my roommate. He said that he played a couple of my songs for his boss and he thought that they were great. He offered to conduct a full string section and orchestrate the album. For my first album, we had used sample strings and I wanted to use real strings for the passion and the quality of sound. We're due to record in the coming months and everything that I asked for is coming into place. I took Joe Vitale's advice by taking 'inspired action.' I recently had the urge to start writing. A few weeks later I had a book that was all about my feelings, experiences and thoughts with the Law of Attraction. I asked for a self-publishing company to appear for me. I came across the perfect one and now I have a book! I thank Joe for his book, The Key; it truly inspired me.

Matt shows what can happen if you let go and trust. He had more obstacles than most to overcome, yet he wasn't concerned with all the things that others thought he couldn't do. He set his intention, took inspired action and let go.

I contacted Joe at the end of 2021 and offered to draw a portrait of him as a thank you for inspiring me through his books. To my delight, he replied and said he would love to have a drawing. I acted right away and sent it to him as soon as it was finished. He LOVED it. I was so happy. One of my heroes loved my work and he posted a photo of himself on Instagram and Facebook. He even tagged me. How awesome!

I sent Joe another email saying how happy I was that he liked it and told him that I'd be happy to do another drawing for him if he ever wanted one. I didn't hear anything else from him, but two months later I found an email from him. He HAD replied, but somehow, I didn't see it. He wanted me to do a portrait of his partner Lisa. He wanted it for Christmas, but by this time it was early January. I replied and said I could get it ready for Valentine's Day. By chance, it was Lisa's birthday at the end of February, so I started the portrait as soon as I could. Both Joe and Lisa loved the final portrait and I feel truly blessed and grateful for the opportunity.

While we were communicating, I told Joe about my experience living with Erb's Palsy and the documentary series I was putting together. I shared a link with him, and he subsequently invited me to be a guest on is TV show Zero Limits Living (www.joevitale.com/zero-limits-living-tv). I was blown away. This all started from sending an email to Joe, offering to draw a portrait for him. I have been a guest on his show and consider him a friend. This is another example of how taking inspired action can lead you to some amazing places. I could have had the idea to email Joe and then brushed it off as a silly idea. I could have thought "What's the point? He won't reply anyway". But what did I have to lose? As Joe says, "expect miracles".

I got the inspiration for this book while listening to Joe's audiobooks. I find it very empowering listening to his radiant positivity on the way to work and on the way home. I have read and listened to the following books by Joe

"The Key"

"Life's missing instruction manual"

"Zero Limits"

"The attractor factor"

"Hypnotic writing"

"Expect Miracles"

"Attract money now"

"The power of outrageous marketing"

"Money loves speed"

One of the books which stood out for me was Zero Limits. When I read this book, something seemed to shift in me. I started to clear my limited beliefs. I'm not saying that I'm totally clear, but I'm getting there. We always have things to clear and clean. If you haven't read the book, I suggest buying it and start using the Ho'oponopono techniques he talks about. One of the messages and techniques to clean is to use the words.

I Love You

I'm Sorry

Forgive Me

Thank You

I am by no means an expert on this technique. I'll leave that to Joe Vitale and Dr Hew Len.

Growing up, my belief was that God is love. God is all loving and if God made everything, then everything is love. If someone upset me, my mother always told me to "Bless them with love." What I've come to realise is that the clearing words Joe talks about became my mantra before I even read his book. I think that is why the book resonated with. I absorbed all of the words in the book and I started to clear even more. It's become daily practice to say "I love you" to everything. I read Zero Limits over 10 years ago, but I have just finished listening to the audio book again. I have noticed subtle shifts over the last few days. I'll give you a couple of examples…

Every Monday morning I'm on traffic duty at school. For 30 minutes I have to stand at the edge of the school playground and stop traffic to allow pupils to cross safely. I always make a conscious effort to smile at the parents in their cars, to try and spread some happiness. Usually, I get one or two parents smile back, but today was different. All week I have been saying "I love you" over and over in my head. Today, while on duty, I was saying it in my head repeatedly, as I smiled at the parents. I would say 50% of the parents smiled back at me. I couldn't believe how many people smiled, compared to a normal Monday. It might sound crazy to some people, but it works.

I have also been trying to clean things from the past. Yesterday, a couple of friends came for lunch and after we ate, we sat in the garden talking. The conversation moved onto the audiobooks I'm listening to, and we discussed them in great detail. Both friends have read many of

Joe Vitale's books and we started talking about 'inspired action' and how the Universe gives us divine inspiration and how we need to trust our intuition. As we spoke, one friend told me about an art class that he runs. He told me about people who have asked to attend his class, but he "didn't get a good feeling about them." As we started unpicking this, it all came down to money. He was worried that this new person would join the class and steal his creative ideas and make money from them, which means he wouldn't have any. I kept on pushing for more… The other friend said,

"Why don't you give this person private tuition?" Which I thought was a great divine idea.

"Yes, possibly", he replied. Everything came back to either stealing creative ideas, not getting acknowledged and lack of money. In fact, he told me of a time last year when someone offered him £75 for one of his drawings.

"That's great", I said. "Did you sell it?"

"No" he replied.

"Why on earth not? The Universe just delivered you some money. Money you said you wanted."

"Well, the lady she said she liked it because the colours would go well in her room."

"And?" I said, confused.

"How insulting is that. She only wanted it for the colours and not the art. So I said it wasn't for sale." I was speechless. I looked at him in disbelief.

"So let me get this straight," I said. "You have a fear of not having enough money. Then, you actually managed to attract some money and then refuse it! You fear the lack of money so much that when money is actually given to you on a plate you don't take it. Your limiting belief of lack is so much that you didn't take an easy £75, because you were offended that someone only wants your work for the nice colours… and then complain about the lack of money in your life!"

My friend laughed and admitted that looking back at the situation it was a silly thing to do. The power of clearing is so important. This led onto a conversation I had with my mother. We spoke about money for a while and then we discussed the trauma of when I was born. She got quite emotional, but because I was cleaning my thoughts, I felt that this was very symbolic. The more I clean, the more the world around me heals. She told me things that she'd never spoken to me about. How the relationships with her parents wasn't great and the names that she used to be called. I spoke about how if someone calls you something enough times, you start to believe it. As we discussed this, everything made sense for us. She also said that when I was born her mum and dad came to see me in the hospital and when they found out something was wrong with me, my mother didn't hear from them or see them for 6 weeks. This was the time that she needed her parents the most, yet they were nowhere to be seen. We will never know why they reacted like that and that is a hard thing to process, but it needs to be cleared. My mother spent hours doing physiotherapy on my arm when I was a kid. Apparently, my grandmother said that she could never have done what she did, to which my mother was really confused. You do everything you can to help and protect your children. There is a lot to clean here, but as she taught me when I was a kid, you need to "bless it with love."

I have taken a lot from the teachings in Joe's books. Without reading his books I wouldn't understand the true power of 'inspired action'. Without inspired action I would have never accepted the job as a teaching assistant, which led to my perfect job. Without inspired action I would never have recorded albums or written this book or started drawing again. Without understanding the teachings in Zero Limits and how inspiration works I would never have been able to hear the Universe give me the idea to do a drawing for Joe. I wouldn't have cleared limited beliefs within myself and attracted my soulmate who is my best friend, and wife. Thank you Joe, for your wise words, and helping me open the doors into a wonderful life.

ACTION POINTS

- Try different clearing techniques such as Ho'oponopono to clear limiting beliefs
- Buy some of Joe Vitale's work to see if they work for you too
- Bless everything with love
- Take inspired action and listen to what the Universe is telling you

CHAPTER SIXTEEN
LIVING OUT MY CHILDHOOD DREAM

I'm a huge Back to the Future fan. I have been for over 30 years. Like many people around the world, I always dreamed of owning a DeLorean time machine. When I was an 8-year-old boy, I wrote to the local car museum to ask if I could sit in the DeLorean they had on show. To my delight they wrote back and said I could. It was a dream come true. It's been on my list of things to own for pretty much my entire life. I have been in a situation where I have been able to afford one, but my greed and my want of more money meant I never purchased one. I kept saying, "When I get more money, I will get one." Sadly, the opposite happened. I lost all my money and the goal of owning my dream car drifted further away.

In the summer of 2021 I had a really crazy idea. Like most of my ideas, I act on them without question. As I mentioned earlier in this book, I teach Design Technology. We have 3 workshops in the department, a CAD room, CNC milling machines, 3D printers and much more. I thought to myself; "What if I started a club at school to raise money to buy a DeLorean and turn it into a time machine replica from the movies." The more I thought about it, the more I loved the idea. The pupils could be divided into groups, they could have separate areas to work on and it could be a cross-curricular club. I could involve the business department, as well as opportunities for marketing and film. I could have a team of pupils create social media accounts, run a blog, Vlog, Twitter, Instagram, TikTok and so much more. I could have a fundraising team, where pupils have to network and find ways to get sponsorship for the project. We would have engineering and research teams and pupils could have leadership opportunities. They could use local university facilities and have a portfolio of work to discuss when applying for university or apprenticeships. This seemed like an amazing idea.

I pitched the idea to my Head of Department. He initially laughed, but as we started to discuss it, he started coming around to the idea. I was on duty with the headmaster early in September and in one of those awkward moments when you don't really know what to talk about, I asked him if he liked Back to the Future. He said he was a huge fan, and this triggered me telling him about my idea. He LOVED it. He had such a grin on his face. We also spoke about the school marketing opportunities and how it could also be a great opportunity to develop and push my subject. So many possibilities. We set up a meeting and I put together a proposal.

A week or two later we all sat down and I went over my plan.

Everyone was engaged and loved it. The only concern was how we would actually raise £35000 minimum to buy a DeLorean. Although I knew it was a lot of money, I knew we could do it. As Marty McFly says in the film, "If you put your mind to it, you can accomplish anything". (Maybe this is why I attract so much, because this has been my mantra ever since I was 8 years old).

I had recently joined the DeLorean owners club. I wanted to find out more about where I could buy one when the time comes and get to know a few people who are also big fans of both the car and the film. (On a side note, by me joining the club, it set an intention, which started bringing me what I wanted). I also joined a wonderful Facebook group called 'Time Machine Builders', who have so much information and advice for people converting their DeLorean into a replica from the movie. I wrote a post on the timeline explaining my hopes and dreams for myself and the team of pupils I will be putting together. A few hours later I received a message that would change my life.

"Hi Matt, I've just seen your post regarding the DeLorean build. I have a DeLorean and was about to commission a company local to me to handle the conversion for me. I would be happy to discuss the opportunity for you and your students to handle this for me and to save you the expense of purchasing a car. I would of course remain owner of my car, but would be happy to agree a price for your students to build my time machine for me, rather than me taking it to the usual car builder. Just a thought. I'm a movie car collector and have a number of other vehicles. Maybe your students could take advantage of these in some way, to help attract attention to the work you're doing. I also own www.its.co.uk I'm sure

I could help with any tools you need for your department. Happy to discuss with you in more detail if this is of interest to you."

Wow! Talk about the Law of Attraction and Synchronicity in action. My jaw hit the floor. I don't think I had ever been this excited. We had just been offered a DeLorean, the money to fund the project and the tools to do it. All of this because I took inspired action. It doesn't stop there either.

I thought it would be a great opportunity to collaborate with some companies. We want to manufacture as many of the parts as we can in school. We have a very well-equipped workshop with lots of superb machinery. I had recently been for an interview for the Head of Department role as my current Head of Department is retiring. I was successful in getting the job and I take over next academic year. During my interview and in my application letter I spoke about the need for a CNC milling machine. This is a pretty expensive bit of kit and the one I had my eye on was £15000. A week or two later I was browsing online, and I noticed one for £4100. I shook my head in amazement. Really? £4100? It looked brand new. I sent a link of it to our DT technician to have a look. Later in the day I heard him discuss it with one of the other guys in the department. It turned out that he had also been randomly looking at it too. We immediately went to our Head of Department and showed him. We set up a meeting with the Headmaster and 1 week later it was delivered. Talk about the Universe delivering!

I was still networking with businesses, and I was looking for a 3D printer that could print ABS and PETG – Carbon Fibre. I noticed a company called FlashForge, so I emailed them and told them a little bit about our project. They replied a week later saying that they loved it. Discussions went on for a while and they agreed to send us a 3D printer for FREE as long as we were the official sponsors for 3D printed parts for the project. The printer arrived last week, and it is incredible. To add to this, I found out today at work that the Parents Association at school will fund ANOTHER 3D printer for the project. That's two free 3D printers in 2 weeks!

We have several big parts of the DeLorean project that are made from 3mm aluminium sheet, which needs laser cutting and then welded. We can weld mild steel at school, but aluminium is not something we can do. By sheer "luck", Coventry University is on our doorstep and they have the facilities to cut our aluminium for us. All we need now is someone to help weld. Last week I received an email from a parent about something completely different and I noticed that he is CEO of a company who specialise in welding, cutting, and milling. I replied and added a little note at the end explaining the project that we are doing. He said he would be happy to help with the welding and it also turns out that one of the people who works there actually came to the school and was in the Head of Departments tutor group almost 15 years go. He's coming in this week to discuss the project. I was walking back to the workshop with one of the guys in the department the other day and with a smile I said, "things just keep falling into place." He replied, "things always seem to fall into place for you Matt." I bumped into the headmaster last week and I told him about the free 3D printers, and he looked at me in disbelief and said,

"How are you doing this?" I know the answer to that I thought.

When I analyse this, what happened was that I set an intention and let it go. I absolutely knew that this project would work, but I wasn't just doing it for me. I was happy not owning a DeLorean for myself. I wanted the pupils to gain experience and have the enjoyment of this unique project. Just getting to work on one and having the experience was enough. Within a few weeks the Universe delivered. My proposal was put together in October. My Facebook post was posted on 18th November. The message offering the car to us was sent to me on 19th November 2021 and we had the car delivered on 21st January 2022. I now have a team of 35 pupils who are working on this exciting project.

When I showed the car to my parents, they loved it. I spoke to my father, and he thought it would be a really good investment. Two months later we found a project DeLorean at DMC Midwest for sale at the perfect price. We had it shipped over and we picked it up from the docks yesterday. That's two DeLorean's in less than a year.

People often tell me I'm lucky. I also tell myself I'm lucky. I believe that we make our own luck. If you have read or watched the Harry Potter books or films, you will be aware of a potion called Felix Felicis, which is a luck potion. At one point in the book, Harry pretends to give it to Ron before a Quidditch match. Ron's nerves disappear in an instant and he does an incredible job at winning the match for his house. He later finds out that he didn't take the potion at all. His mind shifted and his outer world changed, and it all came from HIM. Later in the book, Harry needs to get some information from one of his teachers, but he has no idea how to do it, or where the teacher is, so he takes the potion. When he drinks it, he says, "I just have a feeling that I need to go to Hagrid's house". He doesn't know why, but he had a gut feeling that that's what he needs to do. He follows his instinct, and he gets all the information he needs.

Although this is a fictional story, the principles are the same for manifesting your dreams and allowing the Universe to work for you. You have your own Felix Felicis, but it's not in the form of a potion. We have those gut feelings every single day, but we ignore them. Harry has the feelings, trusts them and acts. When I look at all the things that I have manifested in my life, I have done the exact same thing. I had an idea or a gut feeling, I used inspired action and I received. No wonder people think I'm lucky. I've been using Felix Felicis!

ACTION POINTS

- Follow your instincts (Use your Felix Felicis)
- Let go to allow it to come in
- Want without need

CHAPTER SEVENTEEN
TOXICITY

Do you struggle with relationships? Do you feel as though you go through the same things each time you start a new one? Do you find that you make the same mistakes? Maybe the people at work aren't very pleasant and you can't seem to make new friends. In this chapter I discuss how toxic relationships can have an effect on manifesting things in your life. I have answered yes to all of the questions above. Fortunately, my life is very different now. I have had some toxic relationships over the years. Not just with girlfriends, but with friends and colleagues. The last few years working at my previous school, I became pretty fed up. Some nights I was coming home crying and I didn't know what to do. When I started there, I absolutely loved it, but over time the energy of the school changed. I had a group of friends and we always sat in the same spot in the staff room every break and lunch. It was our routine, but over time it became very negative. It's not always easy working in a school and sometimes it feels as though teachers are at the bottom of the priority list and it's easy to not feel appreciated. More and more work is piled on and there's no time to do anything properly. This isn't in all schools though, there are some incredible schools out there and I feel very blessed to work in one.

I was lucky enough to get some promotions early on in my teaching career and I enjoyed each of the roles. As the years passed, I wanted something more. I wanted to be either Head of Department or Head of Year. My Head of Department wasn't going anywhere, so I was waiting for a pastoral opportunity to come up. Then one day it did. I had been waiting a long time for this moment. It was meant to be. I ticked all the boxes. I could do this job and I could do it well. I studied for the interview and prepared as much as I could. I was so nervous. I HAD to get this job. Honestly, deep down I knew it wasn't right, but I wasn't listening to it. I told myself that this was MY time. I got to the interview, and I crashed. I didn't interview well at all, but I was still hopeful. I was called into a meeting a few days later and I was told that I was unsuccessful. My world just collapsed. I couldn't hold back the tears. I'm not going to go into great detail about what was said, but after that feedback meeting, I wanted to get out of that school as soon as I could. I applied for a job as soon as something became available, and I ended up where I am now. I'm so happy in my school, I can't even begin to explain how different it is. Within a year of me being here, I was promoted to 'Acting Head of Year' and now I will be Head of Department from September 2022. They saw something in me and for that I will be forever grateful. Change is so important. I was in the middle of misery, negativity, and toxic relationships. When I applied for this job, my friends kept trying to hold me back. They were saying things such as, "It's another 15 mins to your journey in the morning", "It's in the middle of the city", "The grass isn't always greener." But I knew deep down it was time. I had to change and I'm so glad that I did.

As the energy changed in my previous school, so did I. And so did the people around me. Every day we were moaning and complaining. No wonder I didn't get the promotion. It was similar to when I was at university and my housemates were constantly moaning about how rubbish everything was. If you're around this talk enough, you start to believe it! I made a conscious effort when I started my new school to remain positive, stay out of the gossip and be kind and happy to everyone I interact with. I became the person I wanted to be.

I've been part of various WhatsApp chat groups over the years and one in particular was toxic. My wife kept telling me that I should remove myself from the group, but at the time I didn't want to miss out on any gossip. Gossip is addictive. Sadly, it's also poisonous. It took me a while to realise this. When I changed jobs, the relationships that I had with my old work friends changed dramatically. In fact, I only see a couple of them now. It was a great opportunity for me to rid myself of any negativity and only be part of positive discussions. For a while I also removed all my social media apps on my phone, as I found they could also be quite negative. That being said, it is all about mindset. If it wasn't for social media, I wouldn't now have a DeLorean at school I wouldn't have all of the Radio-Controlled cars that were donated, and I wouldn't have made the Erb's Palsy documentary. It can be addictive, so it is important to limit time on it.

I've delivered hundreds of school assemblies over the years. Some go really well and others not so well. One day I decided I would base my assembly on how I try to live my life. I called "Mr P's Top Ten Tips for A Happy Life." Here are some of the things I spoke about…

1. **Notice the small things** – If you are travelling to work or school on the bus, look out the window and notice the blessings of the small things in life. The birds in the sky, the leaves on the tree. These small things put life into perspective.

2. **Be still** – Take a few moments each day to be still. This could even be when you are waiting for a bus, or waiting for the photocopier to finish. Take a few moments to breathe and be in the moment.

3. **Be grateful** – There are many things in your life that you can be grateful for. The food on your plate, the roof over your head, the clothes on your back. Each day, before bed, make a list of everything that you are grateful for.

4. **Help someone each day** – Do at least one good deed every day. This could be as simple as opening the door for someone, or giving someone your parking ticket if you have time left on it. Positive actions to others spreads positivity.

5. **Laugh (a lot) – Laughter** is the best medicine. It is one of the

best feelings in the world and lifts your energy. Make sure you laugh about something each day. If you haven't laughed today, find something on YouTube now and lift your spirit.

6. **Try your best** – If you are going to do something, do it properly. Don't do something by halves and then complain you are not good enough or it's too difficult. Aim to be the best version of yourself that you can be.

7. **Listen to your intuition** – The inner nudges, or gut feelings are more important than you realise. Make sure that you listen and act on these nudges as they will lead you to some amazing places.

8. **Be in the moment** – Be in the present and try not to fear the future. If your mind is elsewhere, you are not connected with the now and the reality of what is in front of you. You could be missing something important.

9. **Trust** – Trust yourself and trust in the Universe. Have faith that your prayers will be answered and that you will be given signs to act on. The Universe wants you to succeed.

10. **Ask for help** – It's okay to ask for help from other people, the Universe, God, angels or whatever name you want to put on it. It's okay for people to do things for you and offer advice. Some

of the most successful people in the world have life coaches or business advisors. To be successful, you should welcome wisdom from other people.

I thought the assembly went really well and as the pupils were leaving, I received a lot of "Thank yous" and a couple of kids said, "Great assembly Sir" (which is something that hardly ever happens… kids are hard to impress). As I was leaving the room a fellow colleague said, "Well done… A bit idealistic though." This took me back a little. These are 10 principles that I try and use every day and she is telling me that my life is idealistic. I felt insulted. I also thought to myself, "well she's clearly not happy and not willing to try anything to make her life better." I assure you that if you follow those steps, you will start to realise your potential. You will be happier and you will start becoming the best you can be.

It's important to know your worth. At the end of my time at my previous workplace I felt like I was being taken for granted. I was being asked to do more and more and felt that I was on the bottom of the list of importance. I did NOT feel appreciated in any way. Even all of the extra things that I did above and beyond were just expected of me. People around me were moaning constantly and complaining about everything. I was depressed. I knew that I deserved better than this. I knew what it felt like to love my job. I was just so sad that I once felt like this, but now I resented it and wanted to be as far away from it as I could. I felt sick going to work every day and my anxiety went through the roof.

When I decided it was time to change and leave it all behind, things started to change a little. As I mentioned earlier, when I started my new job, I make a conscious choice NOT to get involved in any gossip. I learned that the hard way. When I changed the inner, the outer changed. Let me explain that a little more. I changed my inner thoughts, beliefs, and expectations. When I did that, my outer world also changed. I took action too. I applied for a new job and got it. I knew my worth and I wanted to be treated better. When I was actually treated better, it took me by surprise. I feel so blessed that I work in a very supportive environment and management really care about their staff. Two months into my role as Head of Year, I was having a meeting with my line manager, and I broke down in tears. We got to the root of the problem, and it was because I didn't want to fail. I didn't want anyone to think I was doing a bad job. I was new to this role, and it was one that I had been waiting for, so I wanted to be amazing at it. I wanted the people who employed me to know that they had made the right decision. I was expecting a lot of myself after only two months. I also brought up feelings of how unsupported I felt in my last job and how I was struggling to adjust to this new life where colleagues and leadership are actually looking out for me. I hadn't realised how much I was still holding on to. As I was crying, I looked at my manager and said, "I'm sorry, I bet you thought I was stronger than this." She looked at me and said, "Your vulnerability is your strength. This is why I wanted you in this role." This was so different to anything I had ever experienced before. I think back to when I was a kitchen designer, and my manager was playing mind games with me about losing my job and I was crying my eyes out. He was wanting me to cry and be vulnerable for his own power. I couldn't quite understand why my manager was being so nice to me.

When we hold onto these feeling and emotions, they can hold us back. As I cried, I let them go and I've not thought about them since. It was cleansing. Letting go of toxic beliefs and experiences can be really hard, but it can be done. There are lots of books and techniques out there to try. You need to find a way that works for you. I find that I journey inwards quite easily, and I reflect on why I'm feeling a certain way. It's not always as straight forward as that, but it's an important part of the way I let go. Letting go is a bit like breaking up with someone. In the moment it's the worst pain ever, but over time it disappears, and you look back and smile about it. I think back to my first proper girlfriend when I was 17. We went out for 2 and a half years and when we broke up, I was a mess. Now at 38 years old, I have a wife and two kids. I bump into her from time to time and she actually worked at my old workplace for a while. We laugh and chat and although we shared those experiences together, it feels like another life. I let go as my life moved on. I didn't have the attachment anymore. As my energy and focus shifted, it led me to someplace even better.

We need to be careful of "attachment." We live in a world full of stuff. Materialistic possessions which we depend on. Many of us can't go a day without the use of Wi-Fi or picking up our mobile phone and we end up wasting time on it. We get attached to these items and really struggle when we don't have them. This is also another form of toxicity. As useful as these items are, we need to be careful with our relationship with them. This may sound a bit odd when I'm writing a book about the Law of Attraction and manifesting your desires. Let me explain…

It's okay to enjoy the things that are available to us, but there is a difference between want and need. When we get to a point when we NEED these items, it becomes unhealthy. I had an interesting conversation with a couple of pupils last week. I said that I spent 4 weeks in jungle in Ecuador several years ago. I couldn't believe what they asked me.

"Why did you do that? What did you do without Wi-Fi?" they said.

"That was the point. I didn't want electricity or technology. I wanted a real experience and to learn a bit about myself and the culture." I replied

"Why though?"

They couldn't understand. They even told me that there is no way they could go a day, let alone a month without their phone.

In 2016, I was part of a team of 4 teachers who took 40 pupils on a month-long expedition to Ecuador and the Galapagos. It was an incredible experience. Exhausting, emotional, draining, and brutal. But incredible. The pupils learned to live without their phones and actually talked to one another, played music, cards and told stories. Many of them understood why it's important to not let technology take over our lives. Don't get me wrong. Social media and technology are very useful. You can make millions online and many of the things I've attracted have been because I've managed to connect with people on social media. I've also been guilty of being addicted to gaining followers, likes and comments. This is when it becomes unhealthy.

There can be toxic programmes on TV, YouTube, social media and even in books. We need to be very careful what we digest. We start to believe that we are meant to look and act a certain way, but this is not real life. If we are constantly trying to look or be like other people, we will never love and accept our true self. Things can stick to us subconsciously and these subconscious thoughts, ideas and beliefs can be hard to get rid of. I've limited my social media use and I try to use it wisely. I've removed myself from group chats and I endeavour to make sure every post I upload is positive in some way. By doing that I am allowing positivity in my life and not getting caught up in the negativity.

ACTION POINTS

- Limit social media use
- Remove yourself from toxic situations
- Surround yourself with positive people
- Avoid gossip and group chats which bring your energy down

CHAPTER EIGHTEEN
FORGIVENESS

Sometimes, one of the hardest things we can do as humans is forgive. I guess it's one of the things that makes us different to the rest of the animal kingdom. We often let our thoughts and emotions get the better of us. I once wrote a blog about how I believe we have lost the ability to use our animal intuition, which is actually a very important thing to have. We live in our heads too much and we can easily be drawn into negative thought patterns. We blame other people for our misfortunes and say, "It's your fault that I'm miserable." We are in control of our own mind and emotions. No other human should hold that power over you. If you are blaming someone else for how YOU feel, then you are giving away your power.

I'm guilty of getting stressed sometimes because I can't always see how the future is going to pan out. I've struggled in some past relationships because I desperately wanted them to work. It felt like I was trying to fit a square peg perfectly into a round hole and it just wouldn't fit. No matter how hard I tried, I failed, and it was getting more and more stressful. As much as we want to understand how the world and the infinite Universe works; we simply won't understand. Our brains can't comprehend such a complex system and although we are capable of amazing things, somethings simply can't be explained. We must have faith. Faith is the key to being at peace in the moment. If you are a non-believer, that is okay. You don't need to believe in a higher power to believe and trust in your emotions and feelings.

The simple fact is that life is random and as much as we try to structure and understand it, we may not always get the answers we want, and we need to be okay with that. It's natural to ask questions and it's a thing that I love to do. I love to look out at the stars and think about how small we really are. When I'm in this state of being, I feel totally connected to the Universe and it makes me realise that the stresses in my life, I put upon myself. The birth injury that I endured is simply one of those things that was meant to happen. I also realised that as random as the Universe is, you can bend it and make it flow through you. With this in mind, it made me reflect on my injury.

I know that I was perfectly fine in the womb and yes, I know that it was "someone else's fault." But I love my life. I do not feel hard done by in any way. Do I actually thank the doctor and midwife for getting me out alive? Yes, I do. Of course, there are times I get frustrated with my arm, but I'd rather that than not be here at all. We can hold so much anger towards other people, but where will that anger lead us? The anger that we hold will only really be detrimental to ourselves. It's a toxic feeling that will only cause more negativity, anxiety, and stress. There are theories that we choose our life experiences and our parents, before we enter the world. Who's to say that I didn't choose to have Erb's Palsy? Who's to say that I didn't decide all of this with my parents before I came here. Maybe we decided that it would be something to help us learn in this lifetime. I feel that I would not have ended up as happy as I am now, if I didn't have this injury. I'm not sure I would have ended up in teaching and therefore, I wouldn't have met my wife and be blessed to have the most amazing family. There is beauty in everything.

The reason we find things so difficult is because we believe that THIS IS IT. This is the only experience that we will ever have and there is nothing more. For some, this is absolutely their belief and who am I to try and convince you otherwise. I'm not one for organised religion per se, but some of the happiest and most content people I have ever met have been religious and people of faith. They know in their heart of hearts that they are going to heaven and that they will see their loved ones again. What an amazing feeling to have. To know that when you die, you will be reunited. There is nothing to fear. To quote Dumbledore, "To the well-organised mind, death is but the next great adventure."

Forgiveness can be such a hard thing to do when someone has caused harm on a loved one. Maybe I'm a bit naïve, but I have no issues with the people that did this to me. I've not known any difference in my life. I was born with it and it's part of my identity. It's a positive part of my identity. I hear more from the parents who are struggling with forgiveness, rather than the person actually living with Erb's Palsy. My wife and I have two children, and I can't imagine how I'd feel if someone injured one of them. I know that each case is different and everyone processes their emotions differently. Our emotions are hugely powerful and sometimes we tune into to the rage that's burning, rather than thinking objectively. I know anger. I've been in places that I never wish to return. It can be dangerous, and you act without thinking. It's important to process the feelings but give yourself opportunities to heal.

As hard as it is, I have learned to say that things are meant to be. Accept what has happened and be in the moment. I completely believe that I was meant to have this injury. It has opened my eyes and heart to so many people and experiences. Some people don't believe that things happen for a reason, but things can happen at random. I like to think that my injury has made me a better person. I often wonder what I'd be like if I had a "normal arm." Would I be as open minded if I was "normal?" Absolutely not. I know myself. I listen to my internal guidance system, and it's led me to some amazing places. I've learned that it's important to let go of toxic things in my life, whether that's people, relationships, jobs, or emotions. Life is far too short to be wrapped up in negativity and anger. It's so important to enjoy it and have a positive effect on others around you, as eventually that positivity will be instilled in everyone. Life is meant to be beautiful. To see the real beauty, we need to forgive ourselves and the people who may have hurt you. If you feel guilty or hold anger towards another human, you will stop the flow of the Universe.

Every religion and spiritual practice teach us to forgive. When we forgive, we get clear, and we can allow love to flow through us. There are times in life when people do the unforgivable, yet we need to find it somewhere in our hearts to be able to forgive them. When we forgive, we are free. We are free from the shadows that hang over us and the weight that pulls us down. It allows us to be truly happy. We often say that we are happy, but deep down, we may not be as happy as we say we are. We are all holding onto something. It could be that you need to forgive yourself. Learning how to forgive yourself, is in some ways, even harder than learning how to forgive someone else. One of the reasons for that is because you understand the reason for the actions you have taken. You know if you did something by accident or on purpose. We all have baggage and we all have history. Learning how to leave the baggage behind, with everything else in the past can be a lifelong journey. Be assured that there are ways to do it and I teach some of these techniques on the 'If I Can You Can Coaching Course' which is available at www.ificanyoucancoaching.comYou must also WANT to forgive and you must do it with an open heart.

When we have managed to get to a place of complete forgiveness, we can manifest things a lot easier. I have been heartbroken in past relationships, and I thought my world was ending. As time passed, it didn't matter anymore. I look back now and I don't feel anything apart from gratitude. I'm grateful because of the lessons that I earned from each situation. I'm grateful because if it wasn't for that thing happening, I wouldn't be in the wonderful place I am now and I wouldn't change it for anything. See beauty in every situation, place and person.

ACTION POINTS

- Learn to forgive to allow the Law of Attraction to work
- Release anger
- Let go of any toxic feelings that you carry
- Forgive yourself

CHAPTER NINETEEN
SELF-LOVE

Do you have deep love and appreciation for yourself? Are you at peace with your mind and body? If the answer is no, then keep reading. Confidence can be a fragile thing whether you have a disability or not. It feels as though there are more pressures now than there have ever been to look a certain way. Social media plays a big part in this, but it's not all to blame. Sometimes I feel like we are living life through a filter. We only allow people to see what we want them to see. The picture has been adapted to make it look how we want it to look. The reality is that there isn't a filter in the "real world" and because of this, people start to lose confidence and self-appreciation. If we are not careful, it could lead to more mental health issues and depression. I see it with pupils I teach, and I have certainly been guilty of hiding behind a photo.

One of the problems of living life "through a filter" is that we don't always talk about the root of our issues. We gloss around them and make it look better than it really is. For some, social media, in a weird way has become a place to hide in plain sight. We are obsessed with telling our stories to strangers before we even tell our loved ones. We make it look as though our lives are fantastic, to gain other people's appreciation, or even to try and convince ourselves that it's okay. We take photos of our food, upload it to Instagram, Twitter and Facebook, before we've even taken a bite of it. Why do we do this? Likewise, with holidays and new cars, we are showing the world how good we want to look to others. The real questions are; Why are we doing this? and why do we feel the need for other people's approval?

Maybe we are looking for compliments. Maybe we just want to show people good food and recommendations of products. My worry is that for some people it's a deep-rooted issue of lack of self-love, self-acceptance, and lack of confidence. We are becoming addicted to our phone and when we don't have it in our hand, we feel naked. We are subconsciously adding fear to our own lives, causing unnecessary anxiety and stress.

Some people are definitely using social media in a positive way and I very much respect that. I know that there are really good forums for people to connect (such as Erb's Palsy Groups) and they are a wonderful place to go to share stories and experiences. However, I'm talking deeper than that. I worry that some people are also talking about their issues openly, without talking to someone in person. It's a strange time to live in because mental health issues are the highest they've ever been. People can't seem to talk, yet we have more platforms than ever to express our emotions.

I sometimes struggle with the media and advertisement as more often than not, men and women have to be "typically beautiful." If you sit in the middle of any city and people watch for an hour, you will see how different everyone is. I love the fact that we all come in different shapes and sizes. It makes life so much more interesting, and everyone is so uniquely beautiful. With this in mind, why are mannequins in shops ridiculously sized? Why are all models tiny? Why are male models usually chiselled and muscular? Is that what all men are meant to look like? Subconsciously we are picking up on all these things and when we look in the mirror, most of us will realise that we don't have the "ideal figure or face," which then slowly eats away at us. What does this have to do with the Law of Attraction? When you learn to love yourself, you get clear. When you are clear, you are acting from a place of not needing acceptance from others or worrying what they may think. When you learn to love yourself, you are happy. Being clear and being truly happy allows the Law of Attraction to bring you what you want quicker. But how do we do this?

Beauty is an amazing thing. We see it all the time, but our eyes are being diverted onto what advertising and the media say is beautiful. We are almost hypnotised by this idea of beauty. I could talk forever about noticing beauty in nature, the birds, the mountains etc. However, I want to focus on the beauty within people. You could be the most typically "beautiful" person in the world, but beauty is only skin deep.

We are all beautiful and unique. I've found that once you begin to have true self-love and self-acceptance, as you let your guard down you start to shine and become even more beautiful to others, both in a physical sense and emotional sense. It doesn't matter if you were born with Erb's Palsy like me or any other disability. You have the power to shine and to be your true self. If people can't or won't accept you for who you are then you don't need those people in your life. You don't need anyone else's approval or compliments to make you feel beautiful. There is so much beauty in being a good person with good morals and someone who respects their own body, mind and spirit. If you interact with someone who is full of love and joy, you can feel that beauty. You can feel it in someone's passion for a hobby or a job. You can feel it in someone's sense of humour. Let's not turn into a world where we only see a person's beauty by the clothes they wear and the figure they have. Have you ever paused to think that the photos you see in adverts are edited? How about the fake nails, hair products and make up? Who are those people without all of that? We are all the same.

Love can easily get confused with lust and desire. Again, watching TV shows and movies make us think that love is having sex on the first date. Or it's that moment when someone walks in the room and you just instantly know you are in love. The reality is, that it just isn't like that most of the time. I searched a long time to find my wife and soul mate. It turns out she was right in front of my eyes, and I was too blind to notice. She was one of my closest friends and I didn't even realise. To find her, I need to find myself and that required me to love myself.

Self-love is often confused with ego. True self-love is knowing that you are a beautiful person despite what others think of you. It's holding a deep sense of love in your heart for yourself. It's not about looking in the mirror and thinking that you are better than everyone else. It's about being happy in your own skin, not worrying about acceptance from others. If you accept yourself for who you are, then you love yourself in the true sense of the meaning.

Self-acceptance is also a very tricky thing to master, especially if you have a disability. It took me a long time to accept it. I worried that others may think that I'm different and that THEY won't accept it. Why did I feel like this? It was a pressure I felt, but I can't quite explain where it came from. I used mindfulness meditation to help me, and I often go to sweat lodges to help shift these blocks. Sweat lodges have been a part of my life for over twenty years. For those of you who don't know what they are, let me explain.

The lodge I attend is a community with connections to the Blood Reserve, Canada. The sweat lodges are held in rural South Oxfordshire, UK, and honour the lineage of the Blackfoot Sundance tradition. The ceremony was brought to this land around the year 2000, by a Blackfoot Sundance leader, elder and lodge leader who passed on the tradition over several years. The sweat lodge is an ancient earth-based medicine tradition calling on mother earth, father sky and the four directions to come and help us in a sacred way. The day begins with the fire lighting ceremony so that large stones can be heated. The fire keepers light the fire, and this then becomes a ceremonial fire. We then build the lodge together. The wooden structure is already in place, but we place the blankets over the lodge and collect the drinking water and other things that we need for the ceremony. Once the stones are almost ready, we stand together in a circle so that everyone can introduce themselves. It's an opportunity for people to share what has drawn them to the lodge. People can say as much or as little as they wish, but it's a beautiful time to be there for our fellow brothers and sisters. At this point we get changed into our lodge clothes and enter the lodge. There are at least 4 rounds (sometimes 5). After each round, we come out of the lodge and take time to cool down and drink water before we go back in for the next round. The red-hot rocks are brought into the lodge and there is time for cleansing with sage. Each round has a different theme. Cleansing, love, prayer, and gratitude. We have time to meditate and pray for ourselves, each other, and the world. When the lodge "door" is closed, there is no light, apart from that of the glowing rocks. Water is then added to the rocks to create a "holy vapour" which cleanses our mind, body and spirit. Then, we end the day with a pipe ceremony, either inside the lodge, outside or in the tipi. The pipes are filled with herbs, flowers, and a small amount of tobacco. Smoking the pipe seals our prayers and it's an offering to the ancestors.

People are on their own individual journeys. Sweat lodges have helped me through some dark times and have helped me release toxic emotions. It gives me space to reconnect with spirit, pray and be one with nature. I'd love to see a world where everyone on the planet is happy in their own skin. Where people don't judge and where people have learned to truly love themselves. I believe that this would help bring us a step closer to world peace. If we eliminated ego and the struggle for power and acceptance from others, we would have no fear. There wouldn't be any judgement and there wouldn't be any fighting because everyone would feel an abundance of love inside of them, there would be no need for negativity. We have a long way to go, but I feel that it's getting closer. Gandhi was so right when he said, "Be the change you want to see in the world." We just need to listen and act on these wise words and not be afraid to do so.

ACTION POINTS

- Release the need to gain acceptance
- Learn to truly love yourself. Use the guided meditations at www.ificanyoucancoaching.com

CHAPTER TWENTY
NOTICE THE SIGNS

We can see the Law of Attraction work on a daily basis. We receive signs from the Universe all the time, but we often look right past them. I'm a big believer in animal signs. For example, if a deer runs in front of me, I will go home and look up any symbolic meaning for a deer. A few days ago, I was walking across the school campus. No one else was around and I noticed two doves on the floor in the car park. For many people they wouldn't think anything of this, but for me it is a sign. I looked up what it meant, and it was very relevant for what I was going through at the time.

These signs don't always have to mean anything specific; they could just be something that catches your eye and "wakes you up". Before my son Gabriel was born, my wife and I were walking through the local woods and a tiny white feather fell out of the sky and landed on my wife's shoulder. I couldn't believe my eyes. I had been feeling nervous about the pregnancy but seeing this really helped me.

A close friend of mine lost her mother at the end of 2021. We met 10 years ago on a spiritual dating website. There was a time when we thought we were going to be an item, but we ended up being close friends. There were a lot of synchronicities that played out to make that happen. She is one of the few people who really understands me and who I can talk openly about spirituality with, without being called crazy. Sadly, her mother recently passed away from cancer, but several weeks after she passed to the other side, she started noticing many signs. I received several videos from her showing orbs flying around the room and what looks like white feathers floating down from the ceiling. It was remarkable.

When I started working as a teaching assistant, for around 18 months I lived in school accommodation with several other people. As I mentioned earlier, it was a Catholic school. There is a lot of history to the building and before it was a school it was run my nuns. One night I got out of bed and opened my door to go to the toilet. Something nearly took my head off! The only way that I can describe it was a golden ball, which was about the size of a football. I opened the door and I instantly ducked and covered my head. I looked up and it had gone. I honestly thought that someone had thrown something a me. There were a lot of strange things that happened when I lived there, but maybe that's something to talk about in another book. The reason I'm telling you this is that there is more out there than many of us believe. There are things we can't explain. Many people buy self-help books, but don't reach their goals. They try the Law of Attraction to manifest their goals, but nothing happens. There are a lot of sceptics out there. There are also a lot of people who must have scientific proof that things work before they believe it. It's a lot to ask to just read a book and believe that this stuff works. To allow the Law of Attraction to work, you must trust and have faith that when you let go, the Universe will deliver.

I've always been open minded. I learned Reiki at a young age, studied Tai Chi for a while and practiced meditation. I've attended Sweat Lodges on and off for 20 years and I'm very interested in Shamanic practices. I understand the power of prayer and I have absolute faith in the Universe. It can be a really hard thing to have in such trying times. But I believe that the Universe has my back. I try my best to work with it, rather than against it. I allow it to work with me by following the signs, listening to my intuition, and acting on it. I have done this time and time again and it hasn't let me down. I admit, at times I have had my doubts, but something then falls into place which restores my faith. The Universe can have a funny way of helping you manifest your desires. Did I think I would start writing a book this year? Nope. But here I am. Where will this lead me? I have no idea. I'm just acting on divine inspiration and trusting it.

We must believe. If you don't believe in a higher power, then believe in yourself and your actions. This can be a difficult thing to do at times. Especially if you have a complicated background. You are in control of your own life. From this moment on, know that you have the power to change. You are writing your own story. Your outer world is a reflection of your inner world. Your habits become your reality.

Do one thing today to start making a change in your life. You CAN do this.

As I said at the beginning of this book, there are misconceptions about the word success. We can idolise rich and famous people and think that this is what success looks like. Maybe our view of success is being able to buy the fastest car, biggest house and eat at the most expensive restaurants. Although that stuff can seem appealing, it's not how I view success. I believe that am successful. I have a job that I love and an amazing family. I drive a new car and we can go on great holidays. As a musician I recorded albums. Did they sell millions of copies? No. But for me, the process of recording them led me to a successful career in another field. I love teaching. I'm loving writing this book. Will I class this book as a success? Absolutely. I've written a book! One million copies sold, or one copy sold, it's still a success to me. I'm just grateful and happy to have done it.

We often hear of rich and famous people dying young, who have been on anti-depressants and other drugs. Were they really happy? I don't know. I know of a person who was high up in the music industry, who managed some very famous artists. He told me one day that several of the people he managed would sit and cry in his office, wishing for a normal life. Some people love it, but for some it breaks them. It's appears to me that it's not all it's made out to be. So be careful what you wish for and remember to stay grounded and grateful if you choose to pursue that life. Ask yourself why you are wanting what you want. Is it ego driven? It's okay to want money and everyone should dream big. It is however important to know where the dream has come from. If you feel it's driven by a need for approval, then maybe meditate on why you feel you need approval first. You may find that once you release that need, your dreams will change.

ACTION POINTS

- Notice the signs in your life as they are synchronicities
- Trust in a higher power and have faith that the Universe has your back
- Meditate on your goals and release any toxic feelings

CHAPTER TWENTY-ONE
THE DAY MY LIFE CHANGED

I mentioned earlier that I spent a month in Ecuador with 40 pupils. It was emotional in many ways, but there was one thing which I didn't mention about the trip. Two weeks into the expedition we were travelling to a different camp. We were all exhausted from digging foundations and mixing concrete in the roaring sun. We were split into two groups. I was on one coach with my wife and 20 pupils, and the other coach was in front of us with the remaining 20 pupils and other members of staff. I had my head down listening to my music and suddenly I heard a horn blast. I look up and I see an old man running in front of the bus. There was no time to react. Not even to scream. The man had hit the front of the bus, cracked the windscreen and rolled off the side of the bus. I turned to look out the back window of the bus and he was in the middle of the road with people running up to his body.

The driver didn't stop. He was in shock. My wife and I were trying to calm the pupils down, as many of them were crying and screaming. We kept on telling the driver to stop, but he continued to drive. Several minutes later he pulled the bus over to the side of the road, got off and ran away leaving us there stranded. We managed to catch up with the other bus, but we were left at the side of the road. Everyone was in shock and as members of staff we were trying our best to comfort our pupils. We had just been part of a hit and run accident. We heard from the local police that the man had died. I was trying to comfort people, but I was just as traumatised as the kids. We were halfway around the world. Thousands of miles away from home. We had to essentially be parents for these children to help them through this tragic event.

We got to our next camp, and we had arranged for a counsellor to come and spend some time with the pupils who witnessed the incident. The people at the front of the bus saw everything. It all happened in slow motion. It took me a long time to get on a bus without replaying what happened. The counselling sessions were very useful, but I really struggled. I was keeping myself together reasonably well, but when we started talking about what happened I fell to pieces. I remember being in a small room with around 10 pupils who were really struggling. I originally went in there to support them. I wasn't really going in there for me. The counsellor asked me how I was feeling, and I burst into tears. I had failed. I failed to protect these children. I failed to look after them. My job as a teacher is to protect and inspire. I was assigned to that trip as their guardian and to look after the sons and daughters of our parents and I failed. As well as failing them, these kids are now seeing their strong teacher ball his eyes out.

I tried to explain how I was feeling but it didn't really make any sense. I remember very clearly that we were all sat on the floor with blankets on our laps. As I was crying, one of the pupils next to me put her hand on my arm and rested her head on my shoulder and said, "It's okay sir. It will be okay". This made me cry even more. I was supposed to be looking after her! Not the other way around. In normal times, such contact would not be appropriate. As teachers, we always make a conscious effort to talk to pupils with an open door, remain at a distance and certainly never allow them to rest a head on your shoulder. It lasted for a very short moment, probably 20 seconds at the most, but a simple act of kindness and support meant a great deal to me.

What does this have to do with the Law of Attraction and Synchronicity? Well, I need to tell you another story first…

The year before I took myself off to Peru and, funnily enough, Ecuador for three weeks. When I first started teaching, we had a teaching assistant called Damian who was from Ecuador. He helped support the teachers in the languages department. We got on really well and became good friends. I said that I'd love to visit him when he returns home. A few years later I arranged to spend a week in the jungle on my own and then visit him in his hometown. We would then fly to Peru together, visit Machu Picchu and see where the adventure would take us.

When I got to Ecuador I checked into the hotel and had a look around the local town. I had never done anything like this before in my life. I booked this part of the experience through a specialist travel company. I was part of a group of ten people who were asked to meet in a hotel and wait in the lobby. Our tour guide would then meet us there and prep us for the trip. As I sat there, I looked at all the people walking by, wondering if they were going to join me on this exciting adventure. After a while, more people sat down, and we all got talking. There was a sense of nervousness and excitement. I noticed a petite woman in her early 20's who caught my eye. I didn't think much of it, but a few minutes later she sat down next to me. We started chatting and she was also part of the jungle experience. We instantly got on and we sat next to each other on the 9-hour bus ride into the depths of the jungle.

I'm not going to go into the details of what happened on the first night, but I'll just say that we became an item. One of the other guys I developed a friendship with said, "I knew something would happen with you two, I saw it happen at the hotel." I was intrigued by what he said but didn't really think too much of it. We all bonded as a group. We laughed, shared stories and were excited to be doing something so different to our normal life. We were all there for different reasons. Personally, I needed an adventure. I had been through a lot in the previous few years. I needed to cleanse myself and for some reason, I was drawn to this experience. On the second night I was asked to have a shamanic cleansing ritual performed on me, to which I happily obliged.

On the second day, we had a leisurely boat trip down the amazon and visited an animal rescue centre. I couldn't believe my eyes. The animals were stunningly beautiful. It was a great day, and I learned a lot about my surroundings and the culture. I thought that this was a once in a lifetime opportunity, so I soaked up every minute. Fast forward two years, I'm getting on a boat with 40 pupils and my now wife, I sense a feeling of familiarity. I've been here before I thought. I couldn't believe it. I'm in the exact rescue centre I was at two years ago!

On the third day in the jungle, there was an option to go rafting and experience the rapids. In the back of my mind, I had a sensation that I shouldn't go, but I ignored it and signed up anyway. I'll be honest with you. I'm terrified of water. When we got down to the water and put our life jackets and helmets on, I felt that something wasn't right. I was the first one to be asked to get onto the raft and I sat on the left side. Instantly I felt uncomfortable. I don't have a lot of strength in this side of my body and my balance isn't great due to my injury. I was told to hold onto the ropes with my left hand. I should have known right then that something bad was going to happen. I was feeling it all through my body. Before I could get off, we were floating down the Amazon. Everyone seemed to be enjoying themselves, but I was scared to my very core. We hit a few small rapids and thought to myself, "Ah, if it's like this, it'll be fine." Just as I thought that I looked up and I saw the water crashing around. Panic ran through every vein of my body. Somehow, I managed to hold on and get through it. Everyone was laughing and enjoying themselves, but there was no part of me that was enjoying this experience. I kept telling myself that it would be okay and then out of nowhere I felt a bump…

I was deep underwater. Disorientated and terrified. It all happened in a split second. I was on the raft and in an instant I was underwater. I couldn't work out where I was. Was I facing up or down? I felt bumping on my back, and I realised that the raft was on top of me. I don't know how long I had been underwater, but it felt like a lifetime. I somehow managed to flip myself over and now the raft was bouncing on my face as we were hurtling through the rapids. I started to think that I would never get out and that I was going to drown here in the middle of the Amazon. I was trying to push myself backwards, but the rapids would keep me under. The longer I was there, the more convinced I was that I would drown. Somehow, I managed to resurface, and I took a deep breath and coughed up loads of water. I couldn't see where the raft was. I looked all around in a daze. In a moment of fear, I thought that they had drifted down stream and left me there on my own. Suddenly, I noticed an ore being stretched out to me. Water was flowing all over my face and I was being bounced around like a pin ball machine. I tried to reach out for it and grab it, but I kept missing. I hadn't noticed before, but there was someone following in a canoe to take photos of us. Next thing I know, he grabbed my life jacket and dragged me over the back of his canoe and took me to shore. The raft with all of my new friends followed us. I rolled off the canoe and felt my face hit the sand. I had never been so glad to be covered in sand and feel it beneath my body. I started to shake, and I cried my eyes out. I crawled to a long, broken branch and sat on it with my head down. One of the guys on the tour with me was really supportive and tried to encourage me to get back on the raft. There was no way I was ever getting back on that thing.

I eventually calmed down and agreed to be taken to the other side of the river. I said that I would walk back to camp, as there was no way I was continuing on water. Fortunately, when I got to the other side a man gave me a lift on the back of his motorbike. It was a good job too as I'd lost my flip flops in the water, I had no sun cream, and I was broken. It was also a 20-minute bike ride, so who knows how long it would have taken me to get back, or even if I would have ended up getting back!

I had the weirdest sensation when my head came from under the water. This might sound strange, but I felt that I had popped up in a different Universe. It felt that I fell out of the raft and got dragged under the water in one Universe and when I reappeared, I was in a different one. It felt like my life had split in half. One version of me drowned and died and then there is this one. The one typing these words now. I can't logically explain this, but it felt so real. I wonder if what I described did actually happen. Maybe I did die. Maybe I'm now living out a parallel Universe reality of the version of me that survived. So many amazing things have happened since that incident, I do often wonder if I'm in heaven at times.

I have always been nervous in water. I thought that it was originally because I'm not the strongest swimmer, due to my Erb's Palsy. I know now that it runs deeper than that. When I was around 10 years old, I remember being in a swimming class at school and one of the gap students grabbed me and kept dunking me under water, from left to right. I couldn't breathe and thought I was going to drown. Every time I see photos of a sunken ship I get the feeling of death, dread and fear run through my body. I feel like I'm looking at my own grave. Again, I can't explain it, but it's such a real experience. Maybe I did die in Ecuador in 2014. Maybe I did drown in a shipwreck in a past life. All I know is that when I act on my feelings in my waking life, it has directed me to some incredible places. When my body is reacting the way that it does when I see shipwrecks, I should listen to it in the way I do my intuition, as it doesn't lie.

When we left the jungle, we returned to the same hotel we started in. We said our farewells and I was due to catch a plane to meet my friend later in the day. As I checked out of the hotel, the lady behind the reception desk gave me an envelope with my name on it. "That's weird", I thought. I opened it and read the note. It simply said;

"Be yourself; no base imitator of another, but your best self. There is something which you can do better than no other. Listen to your inward voice and bravely obey that. Do the things at which you are great, not what you were never made for."

The quote struck a chord in me and I just kept reading it. The note was left for me by one of the guys who I was on the trip with. It was the same guy who said he had a vision of me and the woman getting together. I never heard from him again, but I have quote tattooed on my arm as it summarised everything I was looking for in that trip. I hadn't listened to my inner voice, and I nearly got killed. I know I was never made for going on water and I had previously avoided it. I know that I was made to be a teacher. I now needed to listen to inner voice more than ever. I was given a sign.

I checked my phone and I noticed that a guy called Paul Fejtek and his wife were also in the same city as me in Ecuador. I met Paul at a UBPN (Erb's Palsy) Camp in 2009. He inspired me so much. He has the same injury as me, yet he has climbed all the seven summits and has written a book about his experiences. What were the chances of him being in Ecuador the same time as me? Let alone the same part of the city. He was only there for a short time, so we decided to have dinner together that night. It was a huge "coincidence". But there are no such thing as coincidences…

When I got on the plane to meet Damian, I had no idea if I'd ever see the woman I got together with again. I had no idea what was ahead of me when I landed. I did however feel blessed to be alive. After a few hours we touched down and I met up with my old friend. We greeted each other with a hug, and he drove me to his home. His lived in a beautiful house and his family welcomed me like one of their own. His mum was very kind and offered to wash all my dirty jungle-stained clothes for me. I had no idea we were going to go out for a night in the town! I was exhausted and I needed to sleep. We were up partying until the early hours of the morning in a nightclub. This was so far away from my experiences in the quiet rainforest and truth be told, not exactly what I wanted to be doing. But I knew Damian wanted to show me around.

The following day Damian's parents drove us to the airport, and we headed to Peru. Damian had never been to Peru before, so this was just as exciting for him as it was for me. We checked into a hostel and explored the city of Cusco. We knew we wanted to visit Machu Picchu, so we booked in a tour. The next morning, we woke early and headed towards the pickup spot. We had a long 8-hour drive in a cramped minibus and arrived late afternoon. There was a single train track which led to a town called Aguas Calientes. Rather than getting the train, we decided to walk along the track with lots of other excited travellers. It was a very long walk. We were tired and our shoulders were aching from our backpacks, but intrigued as to when and where this mysterious town would appear. It felt like we were heading deep into a jungle. What kind of town would be here? The light was fading, and we had no idea how much longer we needed to walk. All of a sudden, we noticed some light twinkling from a building as we were coming around a corner. We were nearly there. After another half an hour we found the hostel we were looking for. We dropped off our bags and headed out to get some food. We needed to be up at 4 am to start our climb to see Machu Picchu as sunrise, so after we ate, we headed back to the hostel and got an early night.

We woke up at 3:30am and walked to the meeting point. We were equipped with head torches, waterproofs, bottles of water and snacks to keep our energy up. There was an energy around this place which was hard to describe. It was a mixture of the excitement of the tourists, and the place itself. I couldn't wait to see one of the wonders of the world and to pick up on the energies there. It was now 4am and we started to climb. It was a tougher climb than I had expected, but I was determined to get to the top for sunrise, so we pressed on. After a couple of hours, we were there. We arrived just in time to see sunrise over the glorious ruins of Machu Picchu. What an experience this was.

I decided not to have a guided tour. I wanted to explore it on my own and listen to the surroundings and follow my intuition. I sat there in awe for a long time, soaking up the energy and completely amazed by the stunning beauty that surrounded me. A few hours later I started talking to an elderly gentleman who was also on his own. (Damian had decided to explore on his own.) As we spoke, he told me that many years ago he lived in Coventry in the UK. I couldn't believe this. I was born in Coventry and at the time I wasn't to know, but I would end up working at a school in Coventry. Maybe it was an early sign from the Universe. It was definitely a Synchronicity that presented itself. Sometimes these coincidences are simply to show you that you are on the right path.

We spent many hours there absorbing it all, but it was now time to head back to Cusco. We hiked back to the minibus and endured another 8-hour drive back to our Hostel. We were in the middle of the festival season, so there were not many hostels available. We wanted to stay for three days, but could only get two nights which was the Monday and the Wednesday. We needed to find somewhere to stay on the Tuesday. Damian decided he would stay with me in Cusco on the Monday, and then go to see Lake Titicaca on the Tuesday and re-join me on the Wednesday. As much as I wanted to go, I was exhausted, so I stayed and tried to find a hostel for the night. Little did I know that every room in the city was booked up. I couldn't find a room anywhere. One kind lady running a hostel felt sorry for me and offered me a storeroom, a mattress, and a blanket if I couldn't find somewhere to stay.

I went to a local café to get some food and a drink and to work out what to do. I looked up and I spotted some elderly people who I spoke to when we were climbing up Machu Picchu. They had recently retired and decided to go traveling and do all the things they wanted to do when they were younger. I was inspired by them. I had no idea they were coming back to Cusco. What were the chances of bumping into them again? They called me over to their table and we chatted for a while. We were discussing our plans for the next few days, and I explained the predicament I was in. It looked like I would either have to stay up all night, or sleep in a storeroom. By sheer "chance" one of the guys said, "Take our room. We don't need it. We've decided to move on today." I couldn't believe this. I offered to pay them for the room, but they refused. They showed me to the hotel, they grabbed their belongings and went on to the next stage of their exciting adventure. What did I do? I slept. Talk about coincidences. This was incredible and proved to me that the more I notice them, the more they appear.

The rest of the trip was full of little coincidences, guided by my gut feelings. I learned a lot from this trip. One of the biggest lessons for me was that I should ALWAYS listen to my instinct. Something I certainly didn't do when I went on the raft. Some part of me knew that going on it would end badly, but I did it anyway. My ego was taking over. I wasn't listening or noticing the signs. The Universe speaks to us in different ways, but one of the ways that it does it is through divine inspiration and intuition. Many of us have lost this ability, or, like me, ignore it. When we clear our thoughts, listen, and follow our nudges, we will get on the right path. We don't always know where the path will take us and we can't always see it unfold before us, but there will be something beautiful at the end. Much the same as when I woke up at 4am to see the sunrise over Machu Picchu. I didn't know the path that was laid out before me. It was dark and all I had was a head torch to light my way. Some parts of the path were hard work, and some parts were easier. I had obstacles before me and sometimes I wondered if I could even continue. But I trusted. I trusted the path before me, so I pressed on. By the time I got to the end of the path, I was blessed with the stunning beauty and rewards of my faith.

So what does the tragic accident that happened on the trip have anything to do with the Law of Attraction? I never cleared my feelings from the first trip and my near-death experience. It could be that visiting the zoo again and being on the same part of the amazon river, triggered something in me which attracted it to me. I'm still learning and practicing the Law of Attraction. Sometimes it takes a while to understand why things happen. It's only been the last few years that I understand why I have Erb's Palsy. Synchronicity was playing out throughout the whole trip. I was getting signs from the Universe. Some I listened to and some I didn't. When I did, amazing things happened. When I ignored it, the experiences were very different.

ACTION POINTS

- Always listen to the inner nudges
- Act on synchronicities

CHAPTER TWENTY-TWO
A SHATTERED DREAM

I love campervans. I love the freedom they can give you and the laid-back feeling of cruising down the roads at 50mph while everyone else is rushing by in a hurry. Around 12 years ago I was desperate to buy a VW Splitscreen campervan. I wanted to be a surf dude, even though I'm terrified of water and can't surf. I loved the idea of the lifestyle. Somehow, I thought that just by owning a VW camper, I could embody the idealistic laid-back lifestyle. I started doing some research and I browsed eBay and the usual online car sale websites. I found a VW enthusiast groups and went to VW festivals and shows. I made some contacts, and I located a 1964 Splitscreen for sale in Devon (6-hour drive from my house). I asked a friend to join me for the journey and we set off early morning. We eventually arrived at the garage, and we saw this really cool VW up on the ramps. I introduced myself to the owner and told him that we had come to look at the camper. Truth be told, I had a similar feeling to when I was on the raft in Ecuador. I ignored it. I wanted that VW there and then. In some ways I can be incredible patient, but when it comes to wanting to own something, my patience is awful. Luckily, I'm learning to let go and over the last few years, I'm learning to trust and want without need or attachment.

I asked if he could lower the camper down, so I could look in it and have a test drive. He said, "I put it up on the ramps so that you could have a look at the chassis and see how good it is." I wasn't listening, I just wanted the camper. He lowered it down and I told myself that I wanted it, even though I didn't have the money for it. It was £9000 (which is amazing, considering they are worth £40000 now) but I was determined to have it. At the time I was running a business with my dad and I asked him if we could get it. Looking back now, I shouldn't have put him in that situation. If I wanted a VW I should have waited until I had the money, I should have put it on a vision board and worked at attracting it. In many ways I did attract it, but it came at a cost. It didn't feel right. I wasn't trusting the Universe. I just wanted a camper and I wanted it now.

A week later I went back to collect it. As I drove home, I had an odd sense in my body. I wasn't as happy as I thought I'd be. It felt like it was going to cause me a lot of grief. Again, I ignored these feelings and got on with my life. After around 18 months, the business was collapsing and we needed money quick! I put the camper up for sale to try and pay off some of the debt we owed. At the same time, I was also moving house. I mentioned earlier that I was engaged to someone, and we had bought a house together just before the financial issues of the business hit. My financial world was crumbling, but I was also moving in with someone who I thought was the love of my life. Eventually absolutely everything fell apart. We broke up due to many reasons, I sold the camper, and we sold the house. The selling of the campervan was the start of it all.

I found a buyer who offered £12500 for it. I got an amazing deal for £9000 when I bought it and the extra £3500 would help pay off some of the debt, even though we owed a heck of a lot more. It was moving day, I asked the buyer to meet me at a friend's house (I can't remember why, but there was a reason). He arrived with his wife and was excited to be buying the campervan of his dreams. He asked for the MOT certificate, so I went into the glove box to give it to him, but it was the one from the previous year. Where was it? I knew I had it. It must be in one of the hundreds of boxes in the new house. I asked him to follow me to the new house and explained that it must have gotten mixed up while packing. Even though I was convinced it was in the camper. I couldn't find it anywhere. He had already paid me £5000 deposit and he was getting very angry. I explained that I could go to the garage to get another printed, or he could check online to see that it does have a valid MOT, but he refused. I came up with a deal. I asked him to go home, and I will deliver the camper to him later in the day. I'll go to the garage, get a copy, and bring it to him. He reluctantly agreed. I drove as fast as I could to the garage and explained what had happened. They gave me a copy instantly. I phone him back and told him that I have it and I'll be with him in an hour and a half. He said,

"I don't want it anymore. I don't trust you. I want my £5000 back". I felt like the blood had drained out of my body. I was terrified. I phoned my dad and explained. He had the same reaction. The £5000 deposit was gone. It had instantly been absorbed to pay off some debt. I phoned the guy back and he started shouting at me, "I want my money!" I tried to explain the situation to him, that I was about to be bankrupt, and I need to sell this campervan! He finally agreed but said he would only give me £11000 for it, which was £1250 lower than we originally agreed. I was stuck. There was nothing else to do.

I got in the camper and my fiancé followed in her car. Twenty minutes into the drive, the camper broke down. My heart sank even lower. It had NEVER broken down. I had been the length of the country in it, and it never missed a beat. What was I going to do? I promised him I would deliver him a working campervan in an hour and a half. What am I going to say if I phone him now and tell him it's broken down? I didn't have £5000 to pay him back! I was at the side of a busy road, so I opened the door and went to have a look in the engine bay. The battery connection was loose, so I tightened it back up and fortunately the engine started up. I drove for another half an hour and the same thing happened. To say that I was stressed is an understatement. We finally arrived and the look on his face was terrifying. He had £6000 in cash for me, and he counted it out in front of me, with the remaining £1500 next to him. He was buying it for his family. His wife and kids all looked at me like I was a criminal who had conned them. They had a look of distrust and disgust. It hurt me so much because I try so hard to be trustworthy. I didn't know how I was in this situation. I took the money, handed over the keys and never looked back.

I have made some bad decisions by not listening to my intuition. For some reason I thought it would be a good idea to buy another VW campervan. Even though we were in a lot of debt, I used that £6000 to buy a 1970's VW Bay Window camper. What was I thinking? I had it fixed in my head that I needed and wanted a campervan. WHY? I owed money. Why did I do this? I found one for sale in the next town to where I lived and went over and bought it. Again, I knew something wasn't right, but I did it anyway. I took it to a campervan specialist and asked him to look over it and let me know if he thinks it needed any work doing to it. He phoned me back the next day and gave me a list as long as my arm. What was I doing? I decided there and then to sell it. This was the best decision I had made in a long time.

At this point, I definitely had some clearing to do about selling cars. I sold this camper for the same amount that I bought it for. I did say to the buyer that there will be jobs to do on it, but I didn't tell them exactly what. I know, I know, what an awful thing to do. I want to be trustworthy, but I didn't tell them all of the issues. Why? I had a limited belief that it wouldn't sell for the amount I wanted. I was worried about not having enough money. At this time, I also owned a beautiful Mazda RX-8 which I loved. I bought it for £12000 cash the year before and enjoyed every minute of driving it. When all the issues were happening with the campervan, my beautiful Mazda started having issues too. The engine flooded, I had to replace tyres, and parts fell off it. It was only 3 years old. Looking back, I was attracting all these things. The car had trouble starting when it was hot. If I drove it for any more than 5 minutes and turned the engine off, I couldn't start it again until it was cool. I needed to get rid of it before a huge repair bill came in. I listed it for sale and within a week I'd sold it for only £2200. I lost £10000 in 18 months of ownership. Did I tell the new buyer about the issues? No. I felt awful, and I was riddled with fear because I was replaying the scenario of selling the original campervan. I was terrified. Why didn't I say anything? Well, again, I was coming from fear of not enough. I wish I could apologise to the buyer. I have said it repeatedly in my head, I hope somehow, he's picked up on that energy.

I ended up sharing a car with my fiancé for a while, but when we split up my mum and dad took me out to buy one as I needed to get around. I had no money. Although we still owed lots of money, my parents had put a little bit of money to one side to help pay for some of the wedding. They had £900. We went to the local garage and there was an awesome little black Ford Puma. The owner of the garage said that it had just come in and will go up for £900. We took if for a spin and loved it. I didn't have any bad feelings about this car. I had it for quite a few years and really loved driving it. I got more joy from that little car than any previous one that I owned.

How did we get out of debt? Well, it's not the way that I imagined or hoped we would solve the problem. My father's Auntie lived in Cornwall and we visited her ever year on our summer holiday. She passed away at 95 years old and left her house and remaining money to my father and his brother. We had no idea that she left this in her will. The amount left to my father was exactly the amount needed to clear the debt and avoid bankruptcy. I don't know how I feel about this. I'm grateful that we are no longer in debt, but do I wish that my great Auntie was alive? Yes, I do. I am very grateful that she left this money for my father. God bless you and thank you.

I still wanted a campervan, but I just let it go and said, "one day I will own one." We were now debt free and after clearing my personal credit cards with the sale of the house, I had £4000 left. I didn't want to make any big purchases. I wanted to build my credit score and play it safe. A year later I went to a spiritual festival with one of my friends Laurie (He is a very close friend who came into my life via my ex-fiancé. When I moved out the house, she found a housemate. He was the guy who she asked to move in… talk about Synchronicity). This festival was exactly what I needed. We had healing sessions, gong baths, ecstatic dancing and much more. I felt free. When I arrived at the festival, I parked my lovely Ford Puma and set up my tent. Opposite, I noticed an amazing VW T25. It looked awesome. I wasn't normally a fan of this style, but this one was very cool. Over the long weekend, I got talking to people that I was guided to talk to. The first event I participated in was "Laughing Yoga". It was bizarre. When I arrived, I noticed two women and for some reason I felt drawn to them. When I sat down to do the laughing yoga, they were there too. For one of the exercises, we had to team up with someone. One of the women I was drawn to made eye contact with me, so we worked together. Over the course of the weekend, we all got to know each other.

One night we sat around the campfire talking and singing songs under the starlight. I started a conversation with the guy sat next to me and somehow, we started talking about campervans.

"Have you seen my green VW T25 in the next field?" He said.

"That's yours?" I replied.

"Yeah, I'm looking for something bigger though, so I'm going to be selling it."

"How much are you asking for it?" I asked, thinking it would be out of my budget.

"£1500"

"Do you mind if I have a look at it?" I replied, with excitement building.

He gave me the keys and told me that I could take as much time as I needed and to bring the keys back when I had finished. I knew instantly that I should buy it. I didn't have the feelings I had before. I was not worried about it. I could afford it and still have money in the bank. I went back to him and said, "Can I pick it up next weekend? Where do you live? It turned out that he only lived half an hour up the road from me. The following weekend I met up with him and drove away in my awesome VW T25. I asked the VW garage to have a look over it to see if it needed any work and the mechanic said it was great. It needed some bodywork doing, but I could do that myself. I was in love with this van. The energy was amazing, and it just felt right.

I was allowing the Universe to deliver. I wanted a camper, but I wasn't forcing it to happen. I let go and it came to me. I even dated the woman I did laughing yoga with. She lived in Bristol and although we shared the most incredible first date, it didn't work out. I hadn't cleared my energy from the previous relationship, and I had many insecurities that I needed to work on. On our first date we went to see a band called Bear's Den. They blew me away. I couldn't believe music could be so beautiful. I have been a huge fan ever since. Good can be found in each experience if we look hard enough.

I had some brilliant adventures in that wonderful campervan. Two months after I started dating my wife, we decided to tour around France for three weeks. We decided what we wanted to be in the moment and followed our intuition. We covered 3000 miles in three weeks and the camper drove like a dream. We knew we wanted to spend our lives together. A few years later we were married and had a baby boy. We did a weekend trip in it with the three of us and the dog but decided we should probably get something bigger and more modern that I could use as a daily driver. I decided to sell it and look for a modern van which I could convert. I wanted a VW but kept on telling myself they were too expensive, and I'd never find one at the price I wanted. I decided on a cheaper alternative which was a Vauxhall Vivaro.

Again, I was forcing things. I should have learned my lesson. I sold my VW for £5000 and worked out all of the things I needed to convert a Vivaro in a spreadsheet. I spotted a bright yellow ex AA recovery van for sale in Skegness and decided to go and have a look. If I'm honest, I had the same feeling that I had when I bought the Splitscreen, but I ignored it. It's a very long story but this van caused me nothing but trouble. As soon as I fixed one part, another would break. I would spend hundreds of pounds fixing something that the garage guaranteed would solve the problem, but it didn't work. I decided to get a new engine put in, but something still didn't feel right. Even though it was running pretty well. I decided to sell it. I had spent thousands on it, but I knew it had to go. I was honest when I sold it to the guy who bought it. I had learned that much! I lost all desire to own a campervan from this experience and we decided to buy a family estate car and think about getting a touring caravan when the kids are older. I still love the idea of camping holiday's and I know we will have some magical ones in the future.

A year later we decided to buy a twelve-month-old Skoda Octavia estate. Certainly not luxury, but reliable and it would be able to tow a caravan when the time comes. Last month I was driving home, and the engine cut out on me. I thought it was strange, but I started it up again and carried on. It kept happening. What now? We purchased a nearly new car so that we didn't have to worry about getting jobs done on it. I took it back to the Skoda dealership and they fixed it free of charge as it is under warranty. It turned out to be a fault in the fuel pressure sensor. On the way home, I took the wrong turning off the motorway and added twenty minutes to my journey. That was fine. I wanted to listen to more of my Joe Vitale – Zero Limits audiobook anyway. After I came off the motorway, I drove through a village which I drive through every day and noticed a bright yellow van. "That looks like my old camper" I thought to myself. I looked at the licence plate. "Hold on. It IS my old van". I couldn't believe it. "It's still on the road!" I thought to myself. I was in shock. Why did it appear to me? What was the Synchronicity here? I was just retuning from my new car being fixed and I see my old van which caused me so much trouble. I'm still not exactly sure why I saw it. I do however believe it's now with the owner who is meant to have it. For some reason it was not meant for me. I tried to convince myself to keep it a dozen times, even though my gut was telling me to get rid of it. When I made the decision to sell it and when I was truthful, the right owner came along. It looks like it's running perfectly well for him, and I hope that he's enjoying it.

Why am I telling you all of this? I believe there is a lot to be learned from these experiences. We often try to force things into place. We don't trust that the Universe will deliver. I wanted a VW Splitscreen and I wanted it NOW. I wasn't willing to be patient and wait for it. I didn't trust that the Universe would give me what I wanted. I was impatient. I hadn't got clear. I still had negative energy around money. I wasn't honest with the people buying it and I attracted a horrible sale transaction. When I finally let go, I attracted a wonderful VW which felt right. There was no struggle. It just happened how it was meant to happen. I was allowing the Law of Attraction and Synchronicity to do its thing by bringing the right people to me at the right time. By me acting on divine inspiration I received my dream camper. I then took a step back. I went back to my old way of thinking, and I didn't trust that I could get a modern VW at the right price. I was forcing things again and I ended up with a negative experience. To manifest what we want, we need to let go and trust that the Universe will provide. Patience is key and faith is the door. Materialistic possessions are just "stuff" and they certainly don't bring happiness. This is not to say that you can't have fun and have them in your life. Remember to not get too attached to them and want without need. We can't force happiness either. The best things happen naturally and effortlessly.

ACTION POINTS

- Always speak the truth to yourself and others
- Have patience and faith in the Universe. Ask and let go
- Listen to your gut instinct

CHAPTER TWENTY-THREE
LUCK OR CHANCE?

People say that I'm lucky. In some ways maybe I am, but I created the world around me. I'm so grateful for everything in my life. It wasn't easy though. I've been in some pretty dark places and been so low that I've contemplated suicide on several occasions. I've felt unworthy and insignificant. I often see emotions and fear like a huge wall in front of me. We can paint a wall black in one coat of paint. It's easy. To paint the wall white again requires more work. It needs more time and more coats to make it pure and clean again. Our emotions are like this. It's too easy to allow one negative thought to spiral out of control and bring in fear, doubt, and worry. We must choose to direct our attention to the positive and retrain our brain. If people tell you that you are useless on a daily basis, you will start to believe it. If someone tells you that you are brilliant every day, you will start to believe it. Making new, positive habits can change your life. Don't get me wrong. Monitoring your thoughts can sometimes be hard work, but with practice it becomes easier. Reaching your goals should be enjoyable. When we force things, we are resisting.

Do we make our own luck? Do things happen by chance? The answer to both of those questions is yes. But do I believe that the Law of Attraction and Synchronicity are a huge part in it? Yes. This is why I consider myself lucky. I've not won millions of pounds on the lottery (yet), but I have attracted wonderful relationships, cars, people and much more. I'm sure you've figured out by now that I've also attracted things I didn't want. Things have lined up for me and happened by "chance" because I have got in the flow and allowed the Universe to deliver. Am I successful? Yes, I am. I don't mean that in a big-headed way at all. To some people I'm not successful. Am I happy? Do I have enough money? Do I go on nice holidays? Do I have a wonderful marriage? Do I have harmonious relationships? Yes, is the answer to all those questions. Therefore, I consider myself highly successful. Am I a multi-millionaire yet? No, but what more could I want? I have a job that I love, I have the car of my dreams at work and one with my father, I go on nice holidays, and I can afford to buy food and pay the bills and I have a wonderful family. Life is amazing. There's not much more money can buy.

Many of us are so obsessed with money that we think it's the only tool that can make us happy. Sure, money can buy us experiences and new toys to play with. But we can't take that stuff with us when we go. For some people, the love of money becomes too much, and they want more and more and lose sight of what happiness is. Happiness isn't showing off and gloating about your new mansion or Ferrari. It's cliché, but happiness comes from within. Joe Vitale says that one of the keys to attracting things is "to be happy now". I have attracted so many more things in my life when I have come from a place of happiness and joy. When I was in a dark place, I was attracting more dark things. When I changed my thoughts and made myself happy, everything started falling into place for me. The job, the relationship, the car. Be happy now. Be grateful for everything you have in your life. The fact you can drink clean water, shower every day, eat fresh food, have good friends, read a book, watch a film, go for a jog, pat your dog, browse the internet... whatever you have. Be grateful.

We can live in fear of losing things. It's a bit like a dog eating their food. They are desperate to have it. They bark at you, run around to get your attention and when you put the food down, they eat it in a matter of seconds. It could be that the dog is worried that someone will take it away. They don't savour it. We can be like this when trying to achieve goals. We want it NOW! The journey can be the most rewarding part and it can teach you a lot. You set an intention and then take inspired action to reach it. Sometimes it doesn't go according to plan, but you get there if you listen to your instincts. Have you ever been for a drive and taken a wrong turn and found somewhere beautiful you never knew was there? This is the same thing.

I experience the Law of Attraction most days on the way to work. Whenever I see a car wanting to come out at a busy junction, I decide that I'm going to let them out. More often than not, the car in front of me does it for me. I know this sounds silly, but it always makes me smile as I know that I'm in the flow. Remember Felix Felicis that I spoke about earlier in the book. You can make your own luck. Take action and act on opportunities that come your way.

ACTION POINTS

- Make your own luck by getting in the flow of the Universe
- Be happy now
- Be grateful

CHAPTER TWENTY-FOUR
STAYING TRUE TO YOURSELF

What are you going to do today to make yourself a better person? Are you working on becoming the best version of yourself that you can be? How do we become the best version of ourselves? We all have unlimited potential. I have learned the importance of listening to your gut feelings. When we go against these feelings, we are resisting the flow of the Universe and stopping synchronicities appearing in your life. I have also learned that you can't plan how the Universe will deliver things to you. As much as we try to fix things and work out the HOW, there is no way that you can predict the unfolding of events. Did I know this time last year that I would have a DeLorean parked at school? Absolutely not. Could I have forced that into place? No, of course not. There is no need to try and work out the how. Leave that to the divine.

I have many packs of Angel Cards and I went through a phase of using them daily. They are always spot on and tell me exactly what I need to hear. When I was living with my ex-fiancé, I kept getting the "Time to Go" card and I knew exactly what it was telling me, but I refused to believe it. I wanted to make the relationship work. The more I tried, the more issues we had. I didn't want to believe it, but I knew deep down I had to go. As soon as we split up, I never saw the card again.

I went through a phase when I would sing "Feeling Good" in the shower every morning. Even if I woke up feeling a little grumpy, I would still sing it. By the time I got out the shower, I felt more positive and ready for the day. Singing is good for you anyway, but this taught me the power of setting up your day. It's easy to wake up in the morning and think about all the issues you have to deal with and then get stressed before you even leave the house. Choosing your thoughts and putting yourself in a positive mindset is very empowering. I'm not going to lie to you. Some days are difficult. I also listen to audio books now, rather than listen to the radio. It gives me something to focus on and enjoy, rather than worrying about things I need to do. By the time I get to work I am relaxed and ready for the day.

When I set my goals and targets, I found that it was important to not compare myself to others. I have a lot of role models and people who I admire. In the past I have said things like, "I want to be just like him," or "I want to look like him" and then try and grow my hair to look like a rock god. I'll give you an example...

I'm a huge Foo Fighters and Dave Grohl fan. Dave is so humble and insanely talented. He is a phenomenal drummer, guitarist, singer, songwriter, he's seriously cool, a lovely man and he has awesome hair. Therefore, in my head, I want to be just like him. I want to sing in his voice, play the drums like him and have long flowing god-like hair. Truth is. If I grew my hair out, I would look ridiculous. I shouldn't want to look like him. I should want to look like me. I should want to sound like me. I'm hugely inspired by him, but I now use that inspiration to create the best version of me that I can be.

I recently watched Robert Pattinson in the new Batman movie and thought he was incredible. I've watched an interview or two and he seems like a really nice guy. I thought to myself, "he has nice hair, maybe I should grow my hair like his." Hold on… What am I doing? I don't need to be exactly like the people I admire. I'm lucky that I have a good head of hair. My best friend actually told me once that he was jealous of my hair. We sometimes find we want what others have. We want someone else's body, someone else's hair, someone else's teeth and so on. What we are not doing is appreciating what we DO have. There is nothing wrong with looking up to people and learning from them, but wanting to be just like them is unhealthy. You should be just like you. I think back to the tattoo I had. "Be yourself; no base imitator of another, but your best self." I remember watching the X factor years ago and there was someone auditioning who wanted to sound and look just like Brittany Spears, but sadly it didn't sound good. Fair play to that person for having the confidence and belief in themselves to go for it, but sadly people found it funny rather than wowing them with her voice. I'm sure that if she went and did an audition using her own voice and in her own style, she would have been so much better. This is your own story. Let your role models continue on their journey and you continue yours. Enjoy what they do. Use their successes to inspire your own creative ideas. You don't need to do exactly what they do. What you should have worked out by now is that your role models have followed their intuition and their dreams. They took inspired action, which led them to where they are today.

I'm a big believer in the power of meditation. A couple of years ago my anxiety was so high, I knew I needed to meditate more. I started attending the sweat lodge more, but for some reason I felt that I needed to find a drumming circle. After a little bit of research, I found one about an hour from where I live. You can probably tell from reading this book that I'm a firm believer in taking action if you are guided to do something. Sometimes it's good to have a "sacred space." Somewhere you can go that is just for you. For some it could be a hot tub at night, a shed in the bottom of the garden or a specific park that you like to walk around. Having somewhere that you can retreat to is a blessing. Use that time to be still, listen and connect with the divine. It's also a good opportunity to practice self-love and self-appreciation. You know yourself better than anyone. Take the time to get to know yourself even better and enjoy spending time with yourself. If you don't enjoy spending time with you, how is anyone else meant to enjoy spending time with you? Some people are afraid of being on their own, but it is one of the most empowering things that you can do. We don't like the silence as it can bring up our fears, insecurities, and other things that we may have brushed under the carpet. We often keep ourselves busy to help us ignore what is really bubbling under the surface. Being true to yourself requires you to love yourself and let go of any toxic feelings that you have.

We all have toxic feelings. The difference is that some people know how to process them better than others. Some people are able to change their thoughts easier than others. You need to find a way that you can release anything that you are holding onto. One of the reasons I may not have "succeeded" as well as I could have in some areas of my life, such as my music, is because I don't like talking about myself. As hard as that might be to believe (especially as I'm writing a book about my experiences), I find that I get embarrassed. This comes from doubting my ability. It also comes from the fear of people not liking me and the fear of rejection. What if people don't like my music? What if people don't like my art or book? The most confident I have ever been is when I'm drawing or teaching. It may sound big headed, but my drawings are good and I'm proud of them. Even typing that sentence, I feel big headed. I don't want people to look at me and think, "My God, he loves himself. He doesn't stop talking about himself." So, I keep quiet. If people ask me about my music, I quietly say something and move the conversation onto something else. Same goes for my art, books or my Beating BPI videos I make. If I trust someone, or I know someone well, then I may open up a bit more. From a Law of Attraction point of view, this is something that I must work on, because how can I sell my work if I'm unable to talk about it?

By doing this, I'm not allowing the Law of Attraction to work to its full capability. I'm not believing in my products and I'm worried that they may not be good enough. The beautiful thing about the creative arts is that there is something for everyone. Some people love Hip-Hop and some people hate it. Some people love Hardcore Death Metal and some people think it's just noise. There is something for everyone's taste and not everyone is going to want or love your product and that is absolutely fine. It's about finding your customers and the people that do appreciate what you are doing. I need to accept myself for the musician and artist that I am. If I'm proud of it, then I should want people to hear my music, read my books and look at my art. When I release the need to feel loved and appreciated, the more the Law of Attraction will work for me.

I despise lying. I never lie. I think it is one of the worst traits that a human can have. Honesty is the key to any successful relationship or business. If you tell lies in a relationship then it can lead to all sorts of trouble. If you lie at work or with a business, you can end up losing money, sales and respect. When you tell a lie, it feels horrible. Why should anyone trust you if you tell lies? I would much rather someone be brutally honest and "rip the band aid off," than for someone to lie to me. Kids at school lie to me all of the time. I end up finding out the truth in the end anyway and it often makes it even worse for them. We may tell a lie to protect ourselves or to protect our family. I believe in total honesty. If the truth hurts, it means I have work to do, and that's okay. As important as it is not to lie to others, it's important not to lie to yourself. Be honest with yourself about everything in your life. You may be able to lie to someone's face, but you can't hide from yourself.

What are you doing today that is having a positive effect on the people around you? The ripple effect is happening all the time for everyone around you. Could you imagine seeing the ripples? Just like a stone thrown into the water. When you smile at someone, often they smile back. Hold a door open for someone and say thank you to everyone. Positivity costs nothing. Even if you are not always feeling positive inside yourself, think about the ripples that you are causing. You can still choose to be positive towards other people. If you choose to be positive, you are creating habits that then form who you are. Over time, that positivity becomes your identity.

ACTION POINTS

- Choose positivity
- Be yourself and no imitation
- Be kind to everyone you interact with
- Believe in yourself and have self-compassion

CHAPTER TWENTY-FIVE
IF I CAN, YOU CAN

I feel very blessed. I love my life and everything that has happened to lead me here. I can't be angry at mistakes that I've made. I don't believe in regrets. Mistakes are an important part of learning. You don't just sit down at a piano and play a song. It takes time to learn and inevitably you will hit some wrong notes. Regrets can cause you to have limiting beliefs, so it's important to make peace with the past and try to find a lesson within the situation.

I knew that I wanted to be married and a father since I was young. Attracting the love of my life and having a family was more important than money to me. When I was 12 years old, I used to listen to 'Late Night Love with Graham Torrington' on Mercia FM. I would listen to the love songs and dream about my soul mate, somewhere out there waiting for me. Little did I know that my wife was actually doing the same thing only two towns away. I remember taking my sisters' compilation love CD's and listening to the songs over and over.

Having someone to love, seemed like heaven. I wanted someone I could adore and spoil. I wanted to be the most romantic person alive. I wanted to live out a fairy tale love story. Looking back, it was probably a bit intense! I've had a fair amount of girlfriends over the years and each one I wanted to be my soul mate. My life was entwined with my wife's as a child, but I never knew. I would love to see all of the times that we crossed paths over the years. Each year we used to holiday in the same Cornish town called Padstow. We went to schools that were very close and frequented the same bars and clubs when we were young. We have known each other before, and we will know each other again. There is something that draws us together through each lifetime. Somehow, we found each other again and we will in the next life. When you fixate on not having your soul mate, you are slowing down the process of finding them. Trust that you will find each other, act on any intuitive nudges and you will be drawn closer.

The gift of life is amazing. We are designed to have experiences and to spiritually evolve. Through experiences, we can assist the spiritual evolution. We are given challenges and obstacles. Some of us look at the obstacles and stop. Some find a different way to go around them. Some jump straight over. I mentioned earlier that I'm dyslexic. When I was training to be a teacher, I had to pass a numeracy and literacy test before I was deemed good enough to teach. I started teaching in my late 20's and I hadn't done any maths since I was 16 years old. I find writing a little easier and with practice, I have certainly got better. I knew that I could be a really good teacher, but I was getting stressed about these tests. I was thinking, "what if I don't pass them and I'm not allowed to teach?" I invested in some maths books and started to revise. The pass mark was 70% on both tests. I figured I didn't really need to do as much revision for English, so I spent more time on maths. I did a few mock exams and I got 30%. I had extra time in my exams when I was at school. This was due to my dyslexia and processing speed. It doesn't mean that I'm not intelligent. It just means that I need an extra few moments to process the information. The exams were timed and for me, that caused extra stress and pressure which fogs my mind. After a lot of practice, I managed to get my score up to 75%.

The day of the exams came, and I was delighted to pass my maths paper with a grade of 73%. My English however was different. I got 68%. You were allowed 3 attempts at passing the exam, so I booked another one for two weeks later and studied my ass off. The second time around, I passed with 71%. I was so happy that I could now press on with learning how to be a teacher (even though I was actually teaching a full timetable unqualified at the time). I've managed to have a successful career as a teacher, had articles published in magazines and I'm now concluding my second book. I did all this despite having dyslexia. If you have a vision and you want to do something enough, you can make it happen. You may need to work slightly harder than the other person, but you can get there if you persevere.

Although I live a pretty ordinary life to some, I consider myself very lucky and I know that the Universe has my back. Hopefully while reading this book, you can see how powerful our thoughts and actions are. When I step into the flow, it feels incredible. It's very hard sometimes to not want to control a situation, but the importance of letting go, trusting and having faith is paramount when attracting anything in your life. My stories to some, may not be that exciting. You may have noticed that I have attracted many things that I didn't want. That was partly the point of this book. It shows us that what we think about we bring into our reality. It shows you the importance of listening to the inner nudges and divine guidance. I'm not claiming to be a master, but I do know from reflecting on my own experiences, that I have the power to achieve greatness. As do you.

I hope from reading this, you make time to reflect on your own life and to notice all the things that you have attracted. Self-development is an ongoing job and to be good at any job, you need to reflect on what is going well and what isn't going so well. It's the same as when your manager sits you down and sets targets with you. If you have them in your professional life, you should have them in your personal life. In many ways, it's probably more important to have them in your personal life, because that's when you can really evaluate what you want. Do I imagine being a teacher for the next 30 years? No, I don't. As you can tell from reading this book, I love my job and I thoroughly enjoy teaching my subject, but life flows in ways that we can't predict. I never thought I would end up getting into teaching the way I did. Many doors have presented themselves to me and I walked through them with an open mind. What doors await me? I have no idea, but I'm excited for the future and I trust that the Universe will present the right ones to me when it's the right time.

I feel very lucky that I regularly receive divine inspiration. Some of them I act on right away and some I put to one side and act on them when I'm feeling really inspired. Ideas are like seeds. When we sow seeds, some of them take and some of them don't. Some of them grow to be big and strong and some don't. That is the same for our ideas. The seeds don't struggle to grow. They allow nature to do what it does best. It does it without struggle. We need to think of our ideas like this. We can "feed the seed," but ultimately, it's for the divine good as to how that seed will grow.

I'm going to finish with a couple of final examples of ways that I have created my world around me. A while ago I was trying to clear my limiting belief about money. If you are familiar with the Law of Attraction, you will know that you should give money to receive money. When you are in a place of "lack," this can be a really hard thing to get your head round. I was doing the weekly food shop and on the way out of the supermarket there were two people collecting money for a charity. I don't carry cash around with me, so as I passed them I said, "sorry, I don't have any money on me." They replied by saying, "That's okay. We take cards." I took that as a sign to donate some cash. I had just been paid, so I could have donated quite a lot of money, but I only donated £5. The people I donated to were really happy that I did it, as most of the time people don't stop. I tried to do it with an open mind. It's not the normal charity I donate to, but I thought it'd be a good thing to do, and who knows? Maybe I'll attract some myself.

I returned home and my parents had come to see us for lunch. My dad had an envelope addressed to me. I opened it and it was a bill for

£766. What? How has this happened? I'm on top of my money and I don't have any debt. Where the hell did this come from? It turned out that I set up a small pension when I was 18, after we won the court case. I had completely forgotten about it. The annual fees had been coming out of an account which had run out of money. I couldn't understand what was going on. I gave away money, partly hoping I would attract some back and I got a bill for £766. Why?

From what I understand, I gave money away wanting to receive something back. Even though I had a fair amount of money on the bank, I only gave away £5 and in the back of my head, I didn't want to do it. I wanted to donate to a charity that I wanted, not a random one in the supermarket. So what happened? I attracted the bill. I wasn't coming from a place of abundance, and I wasn't doing it for a pure reason. I did it for my own selfish reasons and the lack came back to me.

When my wife and I got together, we knew that we wanted children. After a couple of years of marriage, we decided to try for a baby. We were ignorant to how long that it can take some couples. We just assumed that it would happen quickly. After almost a year of trying, we didn't have any luck. We decided to get some tests done to see why it wasn't happening for us. We really wanted it to happen and each month we were doing pregnancy tests and getting upset when it was negative. When we decided to go to the doctor, we let go and said, "if it happens, it happens." I went for my tests and Kate went for hers.

A couple of weeks later, I was downstairs, and I heard Kate say, "Uhm… Matt!" I rushed to the bottom of the stairs, and she was there with a positive pregnancy test. We were speechless. The next day Kate had the appointment with the doctor to get the results. The doctor said, "there are a few issues here. There's a chance that this may not happen. Keep trying." Kate replied and said, "I took a test yesterday and I'm pregnant." The doctor looked in shock and asked, "Without IVF?" We now have two happy, healthy boys. The second pregnancy happened in 2 months.

I believe that when we let go of the need to get pregnant and handed it over to the divine, we cleared our beliefs and got pregnant straight away. The doctor was in shock when we told her that we tested positive. Miracles can indeed happen, and we have no limits to our potential. You can use the Law of Attraction for any aspect of your life. I certainly learned a few tough lessons the hard way. I had no idea why I was attracting some of the negativity into my life, but once I became aware, my life shifted. Be careful what you focus on. Do it for the best intention for you and those around you. When you want something in your life, attract it without need. Be happy now and be grateful for everything in your life. Ask the Universe to help you and look out for the signs. Look out for synchronicities and act on them to create more coincidences. The Universe is ready to help you. Step into the flow and live your best life.

I have always believed that I can do anything. At times, I get frustrated, but I know deep down I can do it. With enough practice and patience, you can do anything. When I watched the movie The Matrix for the first time, I believed that I could be like Neo. I believed that we could bend space and time and move things with the power of our minds. I still do. You mind is more powerful than you know. When we learn to unlock its true power, the world will be a different place. Many years ago, I met Uri Geller, who is known for his ability to bend spoons. After his show, I went home and decided to pick up a spoon and try it. To my amazement, the metal between my fingers felt like plastic. With ease I managed to bend solid spoons with no effort at all. I know this sounds bonkers, but it's God's honest truth. Remember. I don't lie. I went through a few weeks of being able to do it, but it suddenly stopped. I'm not sure why, but I wasn't able to do it again. Maybe it was because I believed people thought I was weird and my need for approval stopped my flow. I believe the energy that we have can be used for all sorts of things.

Earlier in the book I spoke about the balls of energy I get when I meditate and how my friend felt that energy in my hands. This is a very real thing. We see this energy in use when people do the "1 inch punch" or punch through bricks. I said earlier that we are all vibrating, and we are all energy. We can learn to use this energy and channel it into anything we want to do, be or have.

When my grandmother was in her last few days on this earth, my mum and I somehow developed an ability to talk without speaking. Again, this only happened for a very short time and then it stopped. We tested it by drawing something on a piece of paper and we would project the image to the other person. I'd say that 80% of the time we got it right. I don't know if it had anything to do with my grandmother passing, but again, it was a very real experience. There is so much that we can't explain.

As I finish this book, I urge you to keep an open mind. It's okay to question. In fact, it's important to question, but don't dismiss things. Not everything has to be proved. Not everything has to have a scientific explanation. I have experienced many things in life that I cannot explain, but that doesn't mean that they didn't happen. We are evolving spiritually and your connection to the Universe is an important part of your journey. To connect with the Universe, you must also connect with yourself. To love yourself is to love the Universe. To love the Universe is to love all things that have been, will be and is. Love is the ultimate goal and you can find an abundance of it within.

ACTION POINTS

- Evaluate your life
- Set yourself targets
- Keep an open mind

CHAPTER TWENTY-SIX
EXERCISES TO TRY

Do you want to manifest more in your life? Do you want to understand who you are and be at peace with it? I have created a coaching course called 'If I Can You Can Coaching,' which is designed to help you on your path to self-love, peace and happiness. I have included some brief exercises here, but we explore these and much more on the course. To sign up, please visit www.ificanyoucancoaching.com I have used these exercises in my life, and I believe that they can help us get clear and realise what we want and help us manifest our dreams.

- Meditate on you desires
- Find somewhere quiet
- Close your eyes and focus your spotlight of attention on your breathing

- Feel your body relax and your breathing slow down
- Picture clearly that which you desire. See every little detail of it
- Connect with it emotionally and spiritually
- Feel your desires are real and that you have them now, in this moment
- Enjoy the feeling and embrace it for as long as you want
- Open your eyes and know that your desire is yours
- Let go of any attachment to it
- Thank the Universe

Write down a script of your dreams

- Write down a list of things that you want. Start by saying, "I welcome _____ in my life. That or something better
- Write down how it FEELS to have them. Write down all the little details that you sense in your body.
- Meditate over them.
- Be grateful for what you have now. Reflect on the things that you have in your life now and feel a deep sense of love and gratitude for them. Be happy now.
- Thank the Universe with all of your heart and love. Say thank you over and over and mean it each time you say it.
- Let go. Know that it is done and have faith that the Universe is working on it.
- Allow the Universe to deliver. Look out for signs and nudges. Remember to act on them, as this is the Universe talking to you.

Use the guidance below and fill in the blanks

I welcome

_____

_____

_____ into my life. This or something better.

Thank you for

_____

_____

_____

_____ I feel truly blessed.

Please help me release the toxic feelings I hold about

_____

_____

_____

_____

_____

Thank you for your constant love and support. I love you. Please help me heal and let go of

_____

_____

_____

_____

_____

By this time next year, I welcome

_____
_____
_____
_____

_____ into my life.

Ho'oponopono

I highly recommend buying Zero Limits - The Secret Hawaiian System for Wealth, Health, Peace and more. by Dr Joe Vitale and Dr Hew Len. This opened my eyes to a new way of healing and clearing. Everything is an inside job. Your outer world is a reflection of your inner world. By using the principles in this book, you will see miracles in your life. As I mentioned earlier in this book, I'm not an expert in Ho-oponopono, but I have found using the phrases, I'm sorry, Forgive me, Thank you, I love you, over and over again, it helps you clean. Make them part of your daily ritual. No harm will ever come from saying I love you.

Goal Setting

I have written 5-year development plans at work, I have also done the same for things I want to achieve outside of work. It's important to set yourself goals and work towards them each day. Use the table below to come up with your 5-year plan

Year 1	Year 2	Year 3	Year 4	Year 5

If you are unsure what it is you want, you may have to do some work to unlock your dreams. Use the questions below to help you;

- What don't you want?
- Why don't you want this?
- What can you do today to stop this from happening?
- What would you do if you knew you couldn't fail?
- What is stopping you?
- What can you do today to help you make a start?

I am a believer of structure and routine when working to accomplish a task. I like to be organised and I believe in a tidy workspace. Only have things in your life that bring you joy. If your home is a mess, tidy it up now. If your office is a mess. Tidy it. How do you expect to think clearly if you have clutter around? Once you are ready, start putting an action plan together. You may want to try setting it out like this…

Goal 1	Action Steps	Start Date	Completion Date Target
Write your goal intention in this box			
Write down things that can help you in this box			

Affirmations and Vision Boards

I'm a big believer in having a vision board. They are a powerful tool which can aid the visualisation process. You must remember that you are unlikely to manifest the things on your board if you don't take action. Creating the board is not enough on its own. When you look at the images, FEEL what it's like to have it. Feel it with all your being and know that it is already yours. Daily affirmations are useful as they can help you change your habits. If you say, "I'm a magnet for good things" enough times, you will believe it. When you believe it, you will receive it. If it helps, print off powerful statements and have them around your house. Surround yourself with positivity. Create your own positivity. Be so positive that nobody can bring you down. Radiate love.

I once read a book about how water reacts to the energy around it. When it was exposed to anger, the water crystals changed shape. The same happened for water that was blessed with love. We ingest water every day. If you bless your water and food with love, you will be ingesting positivity. Remember, humans are up to 60% water, so if the book is accurate, we will also change with the energy that surrounds us.

If I Can, You Can Online Coaching

If you would like to develop your understanding of the Law of Attraction and Synchronicity, please visit www.ificanyoucancoaching.com where you can access the online course for this book. Within the course you will learn techniques to help release toxic emotions, how to love yourself and how to set personal goals. It will also give you the opportunity to explore your emotions and learn why you really want the things you do. The course includes access to videos and a downloadable workbook to help you on your way to abundance in every aspect of your life.

Other projects

If you visit my website at www.mattparsons.co.uk you will be able to learn more about the projects that I have on the go. You will be able to view many of the portraits that I have completed and order prints if there is something you like. You can also listen to all the music that I've recorded over the years as a solo artist and with my band. There are links to Beating BPI (www.beatingbpi.com) and the videos that I put together to help raise awareness and money for Erb's Palsy / Brachial Plexus Injury.

Websites

Matt Parsons – www.mattparsons.co.uk

If I Can You Can Coaching – www.ificanyoucancoaching.com

If I Can You Can – www.ificanyoucanthebook.com

Beating BPI – www.beatingbpi.com

Accept / Adapt – www.acceptandadapt.com

Bablake DeLorean – www.bablakedelorean.com

Victoria Parsons – www.victoriaparsons.co.uk

Social Media

Instagram - @beatingbpi / @ificanyoucanthebook / @mattparsonsportraits / @acceptandadaptclothing / @jacklinesband

Twitter - @mattparsons / @beatingbpi / @mattparsonsportraits / @bablakedelorean

TikTok- @beatingbpi / @bablakedelorean / @mattparsonsportraits

YouTube – www.youtube.com/beatingbpi

Look out for the forthcoming book "Be Your Own Role Model" by Matt Parsons

BIBLIOGRAPHY

Zero Limits – Dr Joe Vitale

Expect Miracles – Dr Joe Vitale

Ask and it is given – Esther and Jerry Hicks

The Law of Attraction – Esther and Jerry Hicks

The Fabric of the Cosmos – Brian Greene

The Power of Now - Eckhart Tolle

Harry Potter and the Sorcerer's Stone – J.K. Rowling

ABOUT THE AUTHOR

Matt Parsons was born in Coventry, UK and currently lives in Rugby with his wife and two children. He is currently the Head of Design Technology at Bablake School. When the opportunities are there, he enjoys writing, drawing, making music and restoring DeLorean cars. Matt is an advocate for Erb's Palsy / Brachial Plexus Injury and is spreading awareness through a variety of platforms. He was featured on Dr Joe Vitale's Zero Limits Living TV in 2022 and is currently writing his next book, 'Be Your Own Role Model.'

Printed in Great Britain
by Amazon